# DRAMA FOR ALL THE FAMILY

By the same author:

*For All the family*
*More For All the Family*
*Teaching the Families*
*Reaching the Families*
*Family Worship*
*Twenty Questions on Baptism*
*Prayers For All the Family*

# *Drama for All the Family*

Edited by

**MICHAEL BOTTING**

CPAS

KINGSWAY PUBLICATIONS
EASTBOURNE

First published 1993
Reprinted 1994





The Church Pastoral Aid Society
(CPAS) is an evangelical organisation set up
to support and help local parishes in their work of mission.
CPAS provides materials and training for leaders of all age groups in
the church family, including clergy, housegroup leaders and those
involved in children's and youth work.
CPAS: Athena Drive, Tachbrook Park, Warwick CV34 6NG.

ISBN 0 85476 358 9

Produced by Bookprint Creative Services
P.O. Box 827 BN21 3YJ, England for
KINGSWAY PUBLICATIONS LTD
Lottbridge Drove, Eastbourne, E Sussex BN23 6NT.
Printed in Great Britain

# *Contents*

# *Performing Rights*

# *Foreword*

## by Nigel Forde

Eye surgery, the construction of motorway flyovers, genetic research, maritime salvage operations and the launching of manned space probes are jobs that are undoubtedly best left to the experts. The arts, however, have always been seen rather differently. Since proficiency in acting, painting and writing depends less on training than on individual talent and taste (along with a capacity for hard work and self-criticism) they have always been the domain where the gifted amateur can match and even, occasionally, outshine the professional.

This book is an invitation to members of the local church family to look, perhaps for the first time, at the craft of theatre and see how it can be used to invigorate, to enlighten and to entertain. It is the starting point of a journey which some may decide to leave at the next station, and which others may follow to the end, after which they may begin to map their own journeys through different and more challenging landscapes.

Like Canon Michael Botting, I am convinced of the power of theatre to make meanings fresh and accessible. Sometimes a sketch can make, in a minute or two, a point which a preacher might take half an hour to put across. Actions have always been said to speak louder than words and few will dispute that truth in an age where nearly all our information comes via a visual medium. But there is another side to the coin.

I used the image of a journey just now; journeys move you from one place to another. But there is a form of transport that goes round and round in circles and brings you back to where you started. That form of transport is called the Bandwagon, and there is always the danger of Christians—desperate for new ideas, new approaches, new ways of communication—to jump on bandwagons. Drama is an attractive bandwagon, but if the experiment with theatre discovers no real aptitude, there is no point in forcing it. We are not all actors or writers, and to fool ourselves that we are, or to be encouraged in that belief by the well-meaning, is to waste our time. More than that—it is to waste our true talent which is lying idle while we chase after a phantom.

Many of the sketches in this book are neat, tidy and to the point; some are much less so. But we all have to learn; and the church family should be the ideal place for new actors, writers and directors to take their first steps in an atmosphere of support and goodwill. There is as much to be learned about the Christian life during the creation and rehearsal of a sketch as in the watching of the finished product. Drama, like mercy in *The Merchant of Venice*, 'blesseth him that gives and him that takes'.

So I welcome this book as a source of material for the church family to explore its own potential and test its talents in the medium of drama; still a powerful and relatively untapped store of ideas and areas for exploration.

But the local church is not only a place for encouragement and support; it is also a marvellously friendly place to bury a talent. Our challenge is to multiply the talents—to take our art seriously and use it wisely and with integrity.

Take this book, then; enjoy it, and let it take you as far as it can. Then, if your appetite has been whetted and your creativity awakened, there is a whole world of experience and belief and honest doubt to be explored.

When I look at the history of English poetry, I find Christian after Christian up there with the very best. Perhaps when the history of drama in the twenty-first century comes to be written, the same thing will be discovered. But not if we don't start now.

*Nigel Forde is a broadcaster, writer and poet. He is a founder member and associate director of the Riding Lights Theatre Company.*

# *Notes on Contributors*

**Michael Botting (Editor)** has been incumbent of St. Matthew's, Fulham, St. George's, Leeds and Aldford and Bruera, Chester. From 1984 he has been Joint Director of Lay Training in the Diocese of Chester. He was Chairman of the Committee that produced the CPAS Family Service and edited *Family Worship* (CPAS 1971). He is the author or editor of *Reaching the Families* (Falcon 1969, revised 1976), *Teaching the Families* (Falcon 1973), *For All the Family* (Kingsway 1984), *More for All the Family* (Kingsway 1990) and *Prayers for All the Family* (Kingsway 1993). He has been a member of the General Synod of the Church of England for ten years and spoken on Family Worship issues.

**Breadrock Theatre Company** was an amateur street theatre company which operated in various seaside resorts and city centres in the mid-seventies. In some ways it was a forerunner of Riding Lights Theatre Company in that increasing demands for Breadrock performances encouraged its leaders, Paul Burbridge and Murray Watts, to believe that a full-time professional company might be viable. They gave shows in pubs, clubs, car parks, city squares, prisons, shopping arcades and on beaches around the UK, communicating the gospel in vivid, joyful and moving sketches. Some of these have already been made available in *Time to Act*; those reproduced here have never previously been published.

**Leonard Browne** taught in Bristol where he began to write and perform drama at Christ Church, Clifton. He is now the Vicar of St Barnabas Church in Cambridge.

**Max Carpenter** is an English teacher and Year Head in a large, Devon Community College and co-leader of Culm Vale Community Church in Cullompton. He has written and directed for theatres, clubs, prisons and churches as well as for TV and radio.

**Peter Chantry** trained for the Anglican ministry at Trinity College, Bristol, where he began to write sketches. He worked as Curate at St. George's, Hyde, and now works part-time as Diocesan Youth Officer in the Diocese of Chester.

**Donald Churchman** was Vicar of St. Jude's, Southsea for fifteen years, where he developed a monthly Family Service and introduced dialogue by means of his two vent dolls Jerry and Sue. Later he became Vicar of Christ Church, Cockfosters for twelve years. He has appeared on television many times with his ventriloquil partners.

**Clive Gardener** went to the Lee Abbey Community in Devon in 1992, where he became co-leader of drama and wrote and performed in many sketches. In April 1993 he spent six months at mime school before going to Wycliffe Hall to train for the Anglican ministry.

**Philip Glassborow**, writer and broadcaster, worked for several years with Scripture Union's Sound & Vision Unit, producing videos and audio programmes. He directed the studio and drama sequences in the award-winning *Person To Person* training video, and later appeared as the storyteller in *Joseph*, which received a Silver Screen award. He has written scripts for BBC programmes, and his stage musical *The Great Big Radio Show!* was one of the winners of the Quest For New Musicals and was presented at the Buxton Opera House in May 1992.

**Derek Haylock** is a member of Surrey Chapel Free Church in Norwich, where he is a deacon, a member of the Young Church team and co-ordinator of music and drama in worship. He is a Senior Lecturer in Education at the University of East Anglia, where he is Chair of Initial Teacher Education. His publications include the four collections of Christian drama, published by the National Society, which are listed in the Bibliography.

**Peter Heywood** is the leader of the LifeSpring Drama Group at All Saints Church, Weston, Bath.

**Dave Hopwood** has been writing and performing drama for the past eleven years. For four years he was in charge of drama at the Lee Abbey Community in Devon. He then worked as a solo mime artist, before co-founding the Insight Theatre Company. He trained in mime and physical theatre at the Desmond Jones School in London, and now devotes much of his time to training church members in the use of drama and mime in worship and evangelism. He has written four books of sketches for churches, available from 5 White Rose Lane, Woking, Surrey GU22 7JA.

**Jabbok Theatre Company Ltd** is based in Leeds, West Yorkshire. In their plays they take on a particular problem—a moral, political or spiritual issue—and work towards a response. They sum up their approach like this: Comedy without commitment is escapist. Commitment without comedy makes you want to escape. Jabbok is the name of the brook '...where there was one who wrestled with Jacob until daybreak.'

**Graham Jeffrey** is Rector of Poynings, Brighton. Kevin Mayhew Ltd have published many of his books—see Bibliography.

**Simon Jones** is a Curate at Holy Rood Church in Stubbingston, near Portsmouth. He has helped to pioneer monthly Family Services in schools, to help take the gospel into the heart of the community.

**Stewart Jones** is Priest-in-Charge of St. Luke the Evangelist, Brislington, Bristol.

**Margaret Marr** is Adviser in Children's Work for Chester Diocese. She is a Reader experienced in leading Family Worship, and has written and published within the diocese a number of all age projects and dramas for use in worship.

**Tim Mayfield** trained for the Anglican ministry in Trinity College, Bristol, where he led a street theatre team for two years. He is now Vicar of Christ Church, Pellon, a mixed urban/rural parish on the edge of Halifax. He has written for revues, church services and radio, as well as for the street.

**Robert Meadwell** is a professional actor who has written many songs and sketches. He regularly performs in music hall style entertainment and is often called upon to contribute special material. Collaborating with Philip Glassborow (see above), he has worked on various theatre ventures—both Christian and secular—and several projects for TV and radio.

**Colin Mengell** is an independent Christian artist worker. He spent five years with a Christian theatre company and is, at the time of printing, attending Moorlands Bible College. He continues to run his own ministry, preaching, performing and teaching skills in drama, poetry and juggling to all age ranges. He can be contacted c/o St. Matthew's Church Office, 2 Crescent Road, Ipswich IP1 2EX Tel: 0473 251630.

**Lance Pierson** is a 'freelance wordwright'—a blend of actor, writer, speaker and trainer, for any churches, schools or other bodies who will hire him. Most of his drama work is one-man shows on Christian themes or books of the Bible. He prefers to use other people's scripts; but has on occasion—especially for Family Services and school assemblies—written his own when he could find nothing suitable.

**Christopher Porteous** is Solicitor to Commissioner of Police for the Metropolis. He is also an Anglican Reader at Christ Church, Beckenham and has been planning and presenting Family Services and preaching at them for over thirty years. He worked for a while with others on a childrens' religious programme for Radio London in the 1970s and has since written the words of several hymns and songs published in various books.

**Carl Robinson** went to the Lee Abbey Community in Devon in August 1990 where he quickly became involved in the running of the drama. In June 1992 he moved to Poland where he teaches English and writes and present on Polish TV.

**Stairs & Whispers** is an independent professional theatre company of four based in Ipswich. Since its inception in 1985, it has achieved a cult following across the UK and abroad in schools, festivals, prisons and churches. The company specialises in the use of mime and physical theatre and has gained an excellent reputation for its dynamic, energetic, powerful and challenging performances and exhausting but rewarding workshops. The ever-changing repertoire tackles subjects ranging from AIDS to zits via bigotry, commitment, drugs, evangelism.... Material can be written to order. Tel: 0473 687186.

**Barbara J. Sumner** is a freelance actor, writer and teacher. The sketches in this collection were originally written for Interact Theatre Company: with this company and others Barbara has performed in schools and at Christian festivals.

**Gary Swart** went to the Lee Abbey Community in Devon in February 1990. He developed an active interest in drama and dance and used his skill in guitar playing. He returned to South Africa in June 1991.

**Trapdoor Theatre Company** was founded by Alun John and Rob Lacey. During the four years of 'full-time' ministry Alun and Rob wrote the majority of Trapdoor material, touring with the rest of the team to church and school venues around the country. Since the winding up of Trapdoor Alun John has taken up a degree course in teacher training, while Rob Lacey is pursuing a freelance writing and acting career.

**Michèle Taylor** trained as a teacher in Cambridge where she was active in amateur Christian theatre. She began her professional career in the theatre with Primary Colours and has been working with Footprints for nearly six years producing theatre for adults and children, church and non-church groups. She currently works freelance using her skills as a director, writer, performer, trainer and researcher with a wide range of groups in many different situations. Her work has involved collaboration with such organisations as the NSPCC, Scripture Union and the Arts Council of Great Britain. She co-ordinates the work with under-11s at her own church in Nottingham and leads some Family Services.

**Margi Walker** worked for a time as a chaplain at Scargill House, where she became a deaconess and met and married her husband. They are now based at Chester-le-Street parish church, where Margi is a part-time deacon, in charge of one of the area churches.

**David Williams** is Team Rector of St Mark, Cheltenham. Over the years he has enjoyed using all sorts of visual aids, including both rehearsed and unrehearsed dramas in a great variety of services. He is a member of the General Synod of the Church of England, and his concern about Christian stewardship is seen by his membership of the Central Board of Finance and the Diocesan Stewardship Committee as well as his four-part drama on giving in this book.

**Lucy Willis** moved to the Lee Abbey Community in Devon in 1989 with her husband, Geoffrey, who took up a post there as a chaplain. Lucy played an active role in the dramatic life of the Community, until the birth of her first child in 1990.

# *Introduction*

It was about ten days after our 1972 Christmas Tree Service at St George's, Leeds, where I was Vicar, that I was stopped in the street by a woman from a neighbouring church. She proceeded to tell me in great detail about the talk their curate had given at the family service on the previous Sunday. I was intrigued, for she had just described the very talk I had given on the incarnation to a packed church at our Christmas Tree Service. The talk was to appear the following year in *Reaching the Families* (Falcon) which I edited, but the curate had obviously had no recourse to that, nor was it likely that he could have been present when I gave my talk. On further enquiry it transpired that a member of his congregation, who had heard me, had described it to him so well and he was able to give it so precisely, that my informant could repeat it to me exactly.

There used to be an old army joke about the passing of a message down the line that began as 'Send reinforcements we're going to advance' but was received as 'Send three and fourpence we're going to a dance'! But such a distortion in the conveying of my message had not occurred. Why? I strongly suspect that the reason was because the talk was almost wholly *dramatic*.

Readers can make up their own minds, because the talk is reprinted in this volume as Sketch 1, usually known as the 'Dustbin' talk. I learnt recently that it was still remembered after twenty years, for, when I first gave it in St Matthew's, Fulham, on Christmas Day 1970, the churchwardens seriously wondered if

I was taking leave of my senses! There is biblical precedent for such reaction.

In my book *More For All the Family* (Kingsway 1990) I quote the wise old saying:

I hear and I forget
I hear and see and I remember
I hear and see and do and I understand.

In using drama in a talk all three of those experiences: hearing, seeing and doing, help convey Christian truth.

Of course, drama and religion have been closely linked for hundreds of years. God himself was using drama long before the birth of Christ. In the Old Testament we read how prophets like Jeremiah and Ezekiel were told to act in strange ways to convey a message to their people. Jeremiah, for example, was told to break an earthen jar in the sight of some men and to say, 'This is what the LORD Almighty says: I will smash this nation and this city just as this potter's jar is smashed and cannot be repaired' (Jer 19:11). In the New Testament the prophet Agabus came to Paul, took his belt and tied his own hands and feet with it and said, 'The Holy Spirit says, "In this way the Jews of Jerusalem will bind the owner of this belt and will hand him over to the Gentiles." ' (Acts 21:10–11).

My 'Dustbin' talk seeks to show that the incarnation itself was a drama—God acting out his love before the watching world, and this is implied when Paul, writing to the Galatians, said that before their very eyes Jesus Christ was clearly portrayed as crucified (see Galatians 3:1). The Lord's Supper dramatically illustrates this and further performances were commanded by the Lord himself. Much of the Lord's teaching was illustrated by drama, so that he not only teaches that he is the Bread of Life, the Light of the World and the Resurrection and the Life, but he feeds the five thousand, cures the blind man and raises a friend to life again.

In the Middle Ages religious truth was often conveyed by Mystery Cycles and Morality Plays. In the city of Chester, where I now live, the Mystery Plays are performed on the cathedral green every five years, encouraged by the Dean and Chapter. Indeed, in 1992 the Dean himself and his young son played Abraham and Isaac respectively. Of course, acting can be used for immoral purposes, but so can literature. Just as Christians do not discourage reading simply because some books are pornographic, there seems to be no reason why we should not use acting as a means of presenting the Gospel. Our world knows the power of drama, which is why so much is used on our television screens, including advertisements. Jesus said that the people of light should sometimes learn from the people of this world (Lk 16:8–9).

After all, drama does physically what we all do mentally—we think dramas. Jesus was a superb 'mental dramatist'.

> For anyone wishing to experiment with the communication of Christian truth through the dramatic medium a more authoritative starting-point could not be found. The dramatic parables of Jesus were used because of his deep understanding of people. He knew that whether or not folk would understand the parables immediately, they would remember them—perhaps to understand them more fully later. Life to most people consists of people and situations, and we think in these terms most of the time. Consequently, when Jesus was asked a theoretical question (who is my neighbour?), he did not theorise: instead, he told the superbly understandable and memorable story of a beaten man who was ignored by his kinsmen yet helped by a foreigner.' (From *A place for Drama in Youthwork* published in the CYFA Information Bulletin September 1970 by Robert Cheeseman, now on the staff of Chester College and producer of the Mystery Plays in Chester referred to above.)

Paul Burbridge, Artistic Director of the Riding Lights Theatre Company, who contributes to this book, also underlines the dramatic value of Jesus' parables. As he said in my hearing some years ago, 'The parables are just waiting to be dramatised . . . they are colourful stories that are waiting to be stood on their legs in front of people.' Examples can be found in the various books by him and Murray Watts mentioned in the Bibliography. To gain a deeper understanding of Christian drama, I would recommend that you read the other chapters in those books, and also the following: Andy Kelso's *Drama in Worship* (Grove Booklet on Ministry and Worship, No. 35), Maggie Durran's chapter on drama in her *All Age Worship* (Angel, 1987) and Michele Taylor's chapter in this book, written from the point of view of a member of a professional Christian drama company.

The importance of 'live' drama cannot be over-emphasised.

Paul Burbridge told me some years ago that during a month's evangelistic street theatre his group saw people coming to know the Lord from several different countries around the world as well as from Britain. Those familiar with the radical approach to evangelism pioneered by Willow Creek Community Church in Chicago, USA, will know that part of their weekly Gospel presentation includes contemporary drama. A good book to read on this aspect of drama is *Reaching the Unreached* by Paul Simmonds (Grove Booklet on Evangelism, No. 19). It is significant that in John Finney's book *Finding Faith Today* (Bible Society, 1992), research reveals that 'live' drama is considerably more effective than the electronic media of TV and radio. The whole of page 67 is especially worth reading. John Finney was Church of England Officer for the Decade of Evangelism before becoming Bishop of Pontefract, and his book is based on research carried out by the Bible Society on behalf of Churches Together in England.

This book is primarily about using drama in family services which are intended for members of the whole Christian family, whether married, single or widowed, but where special facilities are also made to help parents and children worship together. I see family services mainly as 'bridge' services to help those considering the Christian faith to progress into the full eucharistic life of the church, so family services themselves should not include Communion, except on very special occasions like Christmas. Most children love drama, as Jesus observed in his parable of the children in the market-place playing weddings and funerals. If we can involve the children in some simple drama, they will probably insist that both their parents come. However, there are certain problems about drama with children in church that must be considered.

## Visibility

The chancel in Anglican churches may be high and open enough not to present any serious difficulties. But bear in mind that the Good Samaritan is sure to be performed some time, and that the man who fell into the hands of robbers needs to be reasonably visible. If you have a good carpenter in your congregation he might be able to construct something that can be fitted on to the chancel quickly and easily, but it must be reasonably strong and easily stored away when not required. If money is available and staging is required for other purposes, say, in an adjoining church hall, then I would say by far the best buy is portable staging made by Merricks Sico Ltd, Henwood Industrial Estate, Ashford, Kent TN24 8DH (0233 643311). The cost of a stage 8 ft by 6 ft by 2 ft high was £662 + VAT in February 1993. Delivery is free. The particular advantages are that not only is this staging very sturdy, but it is very easily erected by one person in a couple of minutes. When not in use it is on wheels and can be stood upright; when pulled down to a horizontal position legs automatically come down as supports, and the wheels lift out of action. I have seen this equipment in use in conference halls, hotels and cathedrals, as well as in one of the churches where I was minister.

The performers must not only be seen, but conspicuously so. It would, therefore, be money well spent to have proper spotlights fitted on some church pillars near the staged area. This may also mean having special power points provided, not only for spotlights but for other visual-aid equipment.

## Audibility

A good amplification system may help and some children may be able to make themselves heard because they have good speaking voices, but in most situations hearing could be a serious problem. For that reason there is much to be said for using mime, accompanied by one or two narrators at microphones. The mimers will not have the problem of learning lines because the narrators, who can be of any age, can read their parts, though of course there must be proper rehearsals of mimers and narrators together. For this reason I have included quite a number of sketches that use this approach, together with a chapter providing simple advice on miming.

Another method is to use mime to a prerecorded tape such as in the story of the Publican and the Pharisee (see Sketch 3).

## Reluctance to act

Although I said above that most children love acting, not all do. So care must be taken not to insist that all the children who attend the family service are forced to act, or some families may stay away—perhaps permanently. On the other hand there may be some budding actors and actresses who simply need some gentle encouragement. We must help them to gain confidence which means not being over-critical or expecting too much of them.

Obviously, it is important that the person in charge of the drama, who certainly does not have to be the Minister, must be enthusiastic and appear confident, whatever may be the reality. The more that actors and actresses can be involved in the sketch from the start, discussing the best casting, for example, the more likely the success of the project. Young performers will need help in expressing feelings as they act—tiredness, surprise, doubt, joy, fear, etc. This will help them to empathise with the deeper truths in the story that they are thinking about and acting out. Michele Taylor enlarges on these in the next chapter.

In this book I have included some sketches that are longer and more suitable for use in school assemblies. I should like to thank particularly the Revd Stephen Ridley, Chaplain of Birkenhead School, and himself a very capable actor, for his advice over what sketches to include with schools in mind.

* * *

In editing this book I have tried to include contributions from a wide selection of sources, as well as all the dramatic material that originally appeared in my book *Teaching the Families* (Falcon, 1973), which has been out of print for some considerable time.

I asked my various contributors to provide material that fulfilled the following requirements:

(1) The message must clearly conform to the teaching of Holy Scripture, though it does not have to be a story taken straight from the Bible.

(2) There must be a limited number of parts and in each sketch the age of the performers should be roughly comparable.

(3) There should be minimal scenery and only a very few props which are easily obtainable. Likewise with costumes.

Concerning costumes, it has been my practice over the years to have some very large cases in which I put any clothes that might be suitable for drama. Some Christian societies have costume departments. The Bible Society did until it moved to Swindon, when it offered me first refusal on the costumes I had regularly hired from it. I still have them. The remains from church jumble sales can be a fruitful source for some clothes, and more sophisticated requirements can frequently be borrowed at no cost. The wig worn by the lawyer mentioned below actually belonged to our local Town Clerk—a practising Jew! As will be seen in quite a few sketches, jeans and T-shirts are recommended where the costumes are not really important.

It is my hope that as a consequence of using this book readers may be encouraged to try their own hand at script-writing. Even if your literary ability is limited, with a little imagination it is not too difficult to adapt a Bible story yourself. See, for example, 'The Man with Four Friends' (Sketch 2). Obviously it would be absurd to have attempted to lower a member of the congregation from the roof of our church, but it seems to me that the script overcomes the problem easily enough. In fact the young man who rushed up the church proclaiming that he was cured, so startled the congregation that even my secretary jumped—and she had typed the script!

On one occasion at Eastertide I asked our Young People's Fellowship, as part of their weekly Bible study, to work out some dramatic episode to use on Easter Sunday to illustrate the resurrection. This meant that they had to examine the biblical evidence, as well as read one or two short books and booklets on the evidence for the resurrection. The final production was of a lawyer interviewing various witnesses.

* * *

How should drama be used in a family service?

(1) If it is very clearly a retelling of a Bible story, then it could be used in place of the Lesson, in the same way as I have frequently used soundstrips (especially those produced by Scripture Union with Roy Castle taking all the parts as well as narrator).

(2) If it is a bit of drama obviously related to the theme of the service, but not specifically illustrating a point in the talk, then it

could come as a special item in the service, probably before the talk and so can then be referred to by the speaker.

(3) It could come at some point in the talk to illustrate a point in much the same way as a verbal illustration might be used.

(4) It could come at the end of the talk in such a way that the congregation are left to make up their own minds as to how to respond without any pressure from the speaker. Robert Cheeseman writes:

> Drama is usually an indirect means of communication; and the value of indirect communication is that it leaves the conclusions to us: if we make up our own minds, the opinions we arrive at will be strong. They will be our opinions, part of our thinking, and therefore normally much more firmly held than any 'secondhand' opinions (those with which we are spoon-fed). Jesus, of course, used the indirect approach a great deal during his earthly ministry (indeed, 'He said nothing to them without a parable', Matthew 13:34).

One person, whose work has not been included in this book, writing to me from evidently painful experience, mentioned that it would be unwise to publish material that has not been tested in performance. I have, therefore, checked that all sketches have been tried and tested before being committed to print. They have, with the laudable exception of three that were specially written for this book by Colin Mengell. However, it is still the responsibility of those who may produce and direct these sketches, under the guidance of the Holy Spirit, as to whether they further the gospel.

Michael Botting
Chester, 1993

# *Drama from an Actress's Perspective*

In 1986, Murray Watts began his exploration of *Christianity and the Theatre* with the statement that 'the Church and the Theatre have reached one of the richest moments in their relationship for many centuries. There has been a renaissance of interest, within churches of all denominations, in theatre as an art form and as a means of communicating the light of Christ to the world'. There are two reasons why I have chosen this comment as a helpful place to begin my discussion of using drama within the church. First, it clearly gives theatre as an art form priority over theatre as a teaching tool. This is important in a book using drama as an audio and visual teaching aid: drama is undoubtedly a valuable and effective audio-visual aid but, as I shall explain later, this is not its primary focus in my opinion. Secondly, five years after Murray Watts wrote his book, we are still in the midst of a 'rich moment', as witnessed by the plethora of books of sketches and advice, and by the preponderance of drama groups within our churches. In other words that interest is still alive and growing alongside a richness relating to quality of theatre.

Why use drama? Particularly, why use it within a family service? Although this is not the place for a full-blown apologetic defending drama in the church, it is relevant to ask these questions.

But first we need to ask what drama actually is. This is by no means self-evident. A play or a sketch is obviously 'drama', but we could also add dramatised reading (for example, as in *The Dramatised Bible*), performance poetry, liturgy itself and even the sharing of personal testimony. I have seen, too, sign language used very simply to add power to words and music. All these engage the audience in a *story*; drama has storytelling at its heart, and any recounting of a story can become a drama to those listening. The story may belong to one of the actors, or an actor may be taking on somebody else's story. In everyday life, we all spend a good deal of time engaging an audience (however small) in our stories.

Clearly, the normal usage of the word 'drama' relates to formalised storytelling, an activity which uses particular skills and abilities and which acquires, at some point, a mystique separating those who 'can' from those who 'can't'. I think it is helpful, however, to take on board a rather broader view since this can encourage creative thinking around ideas for a family service.

Let's be clear that I am here discussing drama as it can be used by people already within a church. Professional help is always useful in channelling ideas and giving confidence, but I am assuming here that, apart from books and so on, it is not readily available.

I would like to suggest three main reasons for developing the use of drama within the church: 'common sense', heritage and theology.

### (1) 'Common sense'

*A Time to Act* must surely appear on the bookshelf of anyone remotely interested in using drama within a Christian context. In the front of this book, Paul Burbridge and Murray Watts include the ancient proverb, 'I hear, I forget. I see, I remember. I do, I understand.' Without reducing drama to the 'sermon with arms' slot, we need to remember Jesus' love for and wise use of storytelling. He saw the value of relating profound concepts to down-to-earth characters and events in contexts which his listeners would understand. It is worth remembering, too, that in using stories, Jesus was following a well-established tradition with many examples from his own Jewish Scriptures. Stories have an appeal and are memorable, especially if enacted, and the experience can be potent both for those watching and for those participating.

## (2) Heritage

We have a fertile and diverse heritage of drama in the church. While it is true that theatre owes its inception to religious ritual, the relationship has not always been good. The early church had a deep-seated suspicion of the Roman theatre with its pagan foundations and therefore drama was shunned, the baby being well and truly thrown out with the bath water.

The Middle Ages saw a resurgence in drama, growing out of religious ritual which was this time expressive of the Christian faith. 'Miracle' or 'Mystery' plays emerged which retold biblical stories with immense insight. These gradually became more colourful and gave rise to pageantry and entertainment which had little to do with their origins within the church.

The relationship between drama and the church is vast and complex, but there is no doubt that the ancestors of modern theatre had their birth within the church. The liturgy, in all its manifold forms, is a 'drama', a symbolic re-enactment of episodes of theological significance perhaps most clearly seen in the rituals of the Eastern Orthodox Church.

I am strongly committed to the view that we should be reclaiming drama, and indeed all other art forms, for God. And this brings me on to the third main reason to use drama.

## (3) Theology

Christianity is an incarnational theology: it is about the Word made flesh, about God getting his hands dirty and involving himself in his creation by becoming a part of it himself. The arts provide a means by which we can tangibly convey that Word made flesh. Drama, in particular, can be a clear 'incarnation' of God's word, as it conveys the truth (concrete and abstract) through the human voice and body.

*'Art needs no justification'* claims Hans Rookmaker in the title of his excellent booklet (now out of print but worth scouring secondhand bookshops for). It is true that in exercising our creativity we are drawing upon and expressing the image of God within us by his Spirit, and celebrating God's colour and vigour. We are witnessing to what Gerard Manley Hopkins has called 'the grandeur of God' which is shining 'like shook foil'. Drama

can not only display that godly creativity but can also enable people to experience and explore it in themselves.

Theologically, then, and remembering the need to redeem drama and the rest of the arts, drama is defensible in its own right and also as a means to an end. In using drama, we portray an essential part of who God is.

Why particularly use drama in family services? It is a medium which speaks first to the child in a person, be they young or old, and is therefore a very inclusive form of communication. A piece of theatre can often be interpreted on many different levels. Some may appreciate it as a piece of art and be edified by it as such; others may appreciate the story and only later come to grips with its implications; still others may respond at a very deep level to something they have glimpsed and may not even be able to articulate.

Drama is then a very important didactic tool, powerfully inclusive in its appeal, and as such it surely reflects the nature of family worship.

How can we use drama in family services, and with whom? Probably the most obvious answer relates to drama by, with and for children. But let's not make the mistake of restricting creativity and spontaneity to children. Given permission and a suitable environment, adults can also become engrossed in drama on their own or alongside children.

Perhaps the two main differences between drama with children and drama with adults is that adults have a whole heap of inhibitions which children have not yet learned, and that adults also have a great deal more experience on which they can draw. Adults can benefit from drama just as much as children can, and using drama may include those normally on the periphery of church activity (for instance, non-readers; also, mime can be very powerful for people with hearing impairments).

### (1) Participatory drama

In other words a piece of drama where the primary emphasis is on those taking part, rather than on any actual or potential audience. It's something of a cliché to say that all children are natural actors; most play comprises re-enacting situations which are familiar or imaginary. Given a sufficiently well-controlled and supportive environment, children can gain enjoyment and learning from trying their hand at acting out situations from the Bible. But there's no need to leave it there as there's plenty of scope for using material from biographies or fiction. Indeed, if you are working with children who are well up on Bible stories, there is a good argument for suggesting that you *should* consider using other stories.

The great thing about play and about acting out situations is that the children can try out different endings and resolutions, and see which is most satisfactory and why. For instance, they can experiment with following Jesus' teaching in a situation and with ignoring it—what happens and why? How might the characters involved feel? If you are not restricted to straight re-enactment of Bible stories, the scope is vast.

Obviously it is important to temper and adapt exercises to the specific context and people involved, but I think it's important to assume a relationship such as that between an extant group of children and the adult(s) responsible for them. Even if someone from outside is called in to lead a drama session, they should be heavily reliant on existing relationships and knowledge.

Using participatory drama is not an easy option: it requires careful preparation and an ability on the part of the session-leader to follow where the group goes with any particular exercise. It is vital that the session is designed to begin at a suitable level and to carry the group towards the drama at an appropriate speed and with appropriate help. For details of structuring such a session, books such as *Footnotes* and *Using the Bible in Drama* are invaluable (see Bibliography). The leader should be sure of what is wanted out of the session, but flexible enough to take opportunities as they arise. Participants should be clear about what is expected of them at each stage—the roles and situations the leader is asking them to explore. Follow-up questions should be carefully formulated so as to bring out the relevant points (and anything else which people may have discovered).

Drama of this sort may take any of the following forms:

(a) The group is told a story and then encouraged to re-enact it in smaller groups, with as much structure as they need (eg. assign characters, talk them through each stage of the story, and so on).

(b) An adult reads a story or narrates it from memory (or, if they are sufficiently skilled and practised, recounts it extempore) and small groups provide concurrent mime-action.

(c) The whole group together participates in a piece of drama as a group exercise. Imaginative interpretation of the story can provide roles for a large number of people—sound effects, music, choral narrative, mime, etc.

(d) The group is told a story and then asked to enter into it, as individuals, with their imaginations. They can be talked through the story and helped to build up the scene in their minds. It may be that they are able to continue the story beyond the resolution they have been given, or the story may be left deliberately open-ended. This has enormous potential, particularly for adults. The scenes can be acted out, allowing more of the truth to be discovered.

(e) As the group becomes more proficient they will be able to take a more active role in controlling their own pieces. Try providing the bare bones of a story, even omitting the context of time and place. For example, reducing a parable to five essential points and seeing how the groups develop it. The chances are that they will come up with something extremely relevant which speaks directly to them and their peers.

Drama of this sort may be used for one-off church family events or for usual Sunday morning groups, with adults and/or with children. These ideas can also be related to whole congregations, especially notes (c) and (d). Note that by-products include a real strengthening of group relationships and mutual respect. Young and old are given the chance to contribute something unique and valuable.

### (2) Performance

This may become more of a possibility when a group has grown comfortable with using drama, but it should only be a stated aim where you are confident that the desired level of competence will be reached. What that level of competence is must be left up to you. There are differing views on whether performance drama in a church needs to be of a high standard or whether God will honour a lower one and use it, provided those involved have done the best they could. I think it is important that you make a decision and don't start using second-rate performance drama by default.

Helping children to perform for each other is hard work, as drama needs to be pretty good before it can engage fidgety five-year-olds. It is good to share work and accept it for what it is—something which a group has worked on for fifteen minutes perhaps, and which therefore won't be of a high standard. But sharing work in a 'workshop' is different from performance, by which I mean a specific opportunity for people to re-enact something for an audience, something which has been rehearsed and improved.

If the performers are children and the show is for the whole church, beware of the 'Aaaah! factor', that tendency whereby the adults become preoccupied with how cute Daniel is, especially when he forgets his lines. The children are there to communicate, not to be sighed over!

Steve and Janet Stickley say in their introduction to *Footnotes*: 'If the creative gifts are handled and channelled correctly, the play itself should ultimately draw our attention to the giver, not to the gift.' This is what drama at its best can do for us in the church. May I encourage you to explore how you may reveal more of who God is to children and adults by using this most eloquent of media.

*Michele Taylor*
*Footprints Theatre Company*

# *The Use of Mime*

Probably one of the best known Christian mime artists in Britain today is Geoffrey Stevenson. He was at one time a member of the late Canon David Watson's team in York and travelled with David on his evangelistic missions. David and Anne Watson encouraged Geoffrey to take up mime as a full-time occupation, and in 1984 Kingsway published *Steps of Faith*, which is a combined work, with his wife Judith, on mime and dance. Geoffrey has very kindly given me permission to include in this chapter much of his writing on mime. Where page numbers appear in parentheses they indicate where quotations come from his book. For a much fuller treatment of mime, readers must study Geoffrey's book for themselves.

As I see it, mime can be used in family services or school assemblies in two ways. One is for a competent mime artist, like Geoffrey, to perform a mime sketch silently, or possibly accompanied by music or sound effects. The chances of having anyone in a congregation or school with the necessary skill to do this is fairly remote, so it means inviting a visiting artist. However, such artists are rare, are quite entitled to receive adequate fees and are not likely to travel to your area to do five minutes' mime in a family service, unless, say, they had been performing nearby the previous day.

This is not really the sort of mime I have in mind for family services, but rather where one or two narrators tell a story and members of a congregation or school mime. As I said in my Introduction, mime has particular advantages because performers have no lines to learn or make audible, and narrators can read their parts at microphones. Geoffrey Stevenson particularly favours this use of mime in church. 'The only question is,' he asks, 'can it be understood? Is the mime clear? If so, then the audience, whoever they are, will have a much greater tolerance for semi-skilled mime than for bad or ham acting—the kind of acting that is recognisable a mile away by everyone except the actors and their mothers!' (p 30)

Geoffrey goes on to explain the unique power of mime and the art of gesture to communicate—engaging heart, mind and imagination. He writes:

> And if this kind of communication is happening, the mimes are speaking directly to their audience. They are revealing *themselves* with faults and failings, to be sure, and in all their humanity—but also as people whom the Lord has touched, redeemed and empowered with his Spirit.
>
> This is sharing your faith. This is being a witness for Christ.
>
> The use of mime, however, even as a tool for Christian communication, does not automatically convert people. It does not make a service 'modern' and relevant. In the end, it is always a sovereign work of God when his Spirit moves in the hearts of men and women. The final aim of mime in church is simply to help open people up to that Spirit.
>
> Mime is an art form which can, like any art, reflect the image of our Creator God, rich in beauty, majesty, grace and joy. As with drama, so mime deals with people and has the potential to reveal a God who is both merciful and just, and who, because he became man, understands our humanity. He has compassion for us, because he knows us. (p 31)

If your local church or school is intending to use drama in its worship, then a group of interested people should gather together well before the first performance to rehearse, and should reckon to meet on a regular basis. As some of the sketches you use may include the use of mime, then some time should be spent on practising miming skills.

The first essential is *concentration*, because that is what makes an audience concentrate. To be involved in what you are doing is involving in itself. The enemy is self-consciousness, and concentration on technique should be done in rehearsal and not in performance. Obviously a performer is aware of himself and his surroundings, but the only thing that the audience should see is his absorption in the situation being mimed, such as eating an imaginary meal. Jesus was evidently fascinated by watching children at play (Lk 7:32). We could learn much from doing the same, for children are normally thoroughly absorbed in their games, which often include spontaneous mime.

## Some general mime exercises

Here are a few suggestions, recommended by Geoffrey and summarised by me.

*Eyes*

One person sits in a chair facing a group and attempts to use his eyes only to communicate an idea, story or event, say a sporting event or waiting for someone.

*The Mirror*

In pairs, facing one another, very slowly move parts of the body—one acting as leader and the other following. It should be done so that an onlooker cannot discern which is leader. Roles should be reversed. Different parts of the body should be used.

*Machines*

This is an exercise where everyone works together. Geoffrey describes it as follows:

> To start: one person finds a strong, simple action while standing, sitting or lying down, which they can repeat endlessly without tiring too much. Invent a noise to go with it, and keep to this repetitive action plus noise at about one beat per second or whatever is comfortable. One by one, the group add on to this with different movements and sounds to accompany them. First find the action—then add the noise. Have one person standing out, keeping time on a tambourine, or the back of a chair. When everyone is a part of the machine, he can play with the tempo. Slow the machine down to a crawl, or speed it up until it disintegrates. (pp 36-7)

The exercise is worth repeating, building better machines that have a wider range of actions. Geoffrey reckons that this is the best one he knows for introducing a group to the concentration and precision of movement, which makes all the difference between a shambles on stage, which is boring and irritating to watch, and a group coherence that must be present in ensemble mime or crowd scenes in a play.

*Bus-stop*

The group imagine themselves in a line queuing for a bus which is expected from a specific direction. Everyone performs a different mime that might occur in such a situation, lasting from 10-15 seconds, such as stepping out to see if the bus is coming and stepping back, then checking money for the fare. Each sequence should be precise and brief and able to be repeated endlessly. It must be the same every time, down to the smallest part, including facial expressions. Get the actions to be silently and simultaneously played out. Then, unknown to those in the total group who are not participating but watching, repeat, but all but one of the mimes freezes. The attention will immediately be focused on the one still moving. On another occasion and with a different audience repeat the procedure, but with only one mimer freezing. Attention will then be drawn to him or her.

## Basic mime techniques and approaches

Believe in the reality of the world you are miming. This will require exercising a vivid imagination, and concentration. For example don't just tug at the leash of any old dog, but feel the leather around your wrist, and pull of a small but tremendously strong Yorkshire terrier named Dennis who has other things in mind than going for a walk. Spend time cultivating your memory of how you actually do normal activities and handle familiar objects. Consider, for example, all the separate movements that go into having a drink from a glass. Having practised them, smooth them out for a performance. Notice how differently you would handle a cube from a sphere.

Character study is all important for the mimer. In fact we unconsciously use our body, especially our head, eyes and chest when we are involved in conversation. Make a point of watching people in the street, in meetings, on buses and station platforms. Note how they wait, walk and talk. Observe people on television, especially with the sound turned down: note the face and eyes and then the whole image the body gives. It is not too difficult to incorporate what you learn into your characterisations in mime, because to a large extent you are doing it all the time. You just need to give more conscious attention to the way people express themselves in the use of their bodies.

Consider different occupations such as bus conductor, teacher, chef, nurse, and mime some of the more obvious actions that will illustrate their occupations. Think about the way people of different ages behave, from energetic teenagers to frail, elderly men and women. Reflect on how you should illustrate the fat person, the intellectual, the tough, the underdog, the proud, the alluring and the hero or heroine.

## Let's pretend

All theatre is pretence, and playwright, actors and audience know it. The mime artist is involved in pretence or illusion, but he is not attempting to deceive. As Kay Hamblin has put it, 'Mime is trickery by consensus.' The audience are not being taken in, but rather are being taken along. However, the trickery or illusion should not so dominate that the message of the mime is missed—a danger that can occur with the use of all visual aids, if care is not taken.

An example of illusion is that of walking-without-changing-place, which is obviously very useful in the small confines of a stage in church or school. Space does not permit me to go into detail here, but Geoffrey Stevenson does, along with other useful illusions in his book on pages 57–66.

The parable of the Prodigal Son provides plenty of scope for mime. Work out the parting of son from father; the kissing of the hand of a loose woman; the wining and dining in a posh restaurant; his removal by a waiter when he cannot pay; his dejected experience feeding pigs and the dawning realisation that his father's servants are better off than he is; his decision to go home; the re-uniting with his father followed by robe, ring and fatted calf; the anger of the elder brother and an attempted reconciliation by the father.

Giving attention to such details is the dramatic equivalent of the masterful story-telling techniques that made the teaching of Jesus so memorable to those who heard his parables. And his parables, as illustrated by the Prodigal Son, just cry out to be mimed. Some fifteen sketches in this book depend on mime, so it is essential, if you are going to include drama in your family services or school assemblies, that serious attention is given to the art. What I have written here is only a starter—I recommend that Geoffrey's book should be purchased, read and *acted* upon.

*Michael Botting*

# *The Use of Puppetry*

A puppet is an animated doll. The amount of animation that is possible depends on the kind of puppet you have. Many people are using puppets today to bring the Gospel alive, especially with children. Several puppets used together are an effective way of dramatising a Bible story. But a single puppet can be used as the second person in a dialogue.

Before we start thinking about the various ways in which puppets can be used, we ought to notice the different kinds that are on the market.

## Different types

### *Stick puppets*

These are very easy to make, as they simply consist of moulded heads on sticks, with clothes covering an unshaped body. It is possible to buy them with mouths which open and close. This kind of puppet is best used when the manipulator is out of sight and the auditorium is not too large. It is best for a Sunday School class rather than for a Sunday School.

### *Glove puppets*

These are similar to stick puppets, except that the moulded head is attached to a glove instead of a stick. The head is hollow so that a couple of fingers can be inserted, and the glove is in the shape of a garment with hollow sleeves for the other fingers. The puppet is

Figure 1

animated by the movements of the fingers. Puppets of this kind don't have to be human representations: some of the best known are animals. The most sophisticated puppets, such as Basil Brush of TV fame, have mouth movements as well.

Again the person manipulating the puppet is best out of sight while another person is actually talking to the puppet.

Figure 2

*String puppets (marionettes)*

These are controlled by strings attached to a wooden crosspiece. They can be made to walk across floors and put into many different postures. Many models are made with mouths which open and close, thus adding to their usefulness.

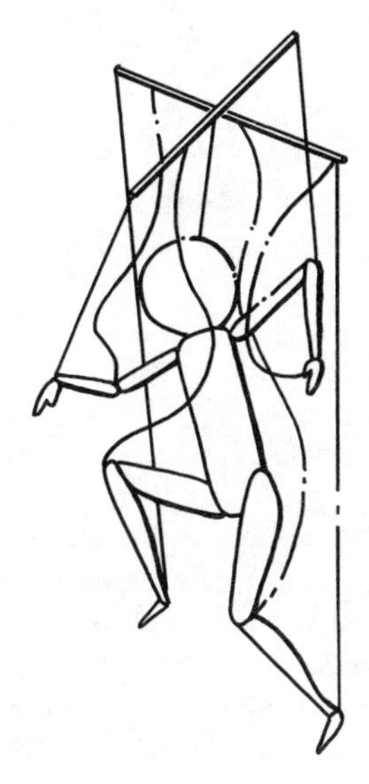

Figure 3

*Ventriloquist dolls*

This kind of puppetry is perhaps the most sophisticated of all. Vent dolls, as they are called, are usually human but not necessarily so. They are created for dialogue, and the manipulator needs to master the art of making his voice *appear* to come from the doll. Their movements can be almost legion. In a simple doll there are two operating levers for the bottom lip and eyelids. In the top professional models there can be as many as seven levers which operate the top and lower lip, eyelids, eyes, eyebrows and even the ears. Add to this the head movements and you have a complete person. They can be made to operate with either hand.

Figure 4

**Which is best?**

Several factors need to be borne in mind: How big is the church or church hall? Is it a team or one-man operation? How much time is there for preparation? Which is the most effective way of getting what I want to say across to the congregation?

To dramatise a Bible story, the best way is to use string puppets with some kind of backcloth and stage. This ought to be arranged so the operators cannot be seen. Quite a number of helpers will be needed, not only in the actual presentation but also in the preparation. Appropriate clothes have to be made and a great deal of time spent in practising the postures and movements of the different characters. A taped music background is helpful, but then timing becomes an important factor. It is embarrassing to have to stop the presentation in order to untangle puppet strings. If the puppets have mouth movements, then voices too can be put on tape and a complete story presented without offstage voices. The main problem with this method is the time it takes to prepare and the number of people involved.

Probably the best use for such puppets is the special occasion. One big difficulty is presenting them in such a way that everybody can see what is going on. Stick and glove puppets can be used in the same way, perhaps getting the Sunday School children to help. Sometimes the top of a piano can be used as a stage.

The most effective form of puppetry for a family service is that which involves dialogue. This is not a visual aid in the generally accepted sense of the word. It is just another way of saying something. This method does not necessarily involve ventriloquism. (Ventriloquism is the art of making another person or thing appear to speak. This gives the impression of throwing your voice. But it is only an impression: you do not, in fact, throw your voice at all. It is a delusion like a conjuring trick or sleight of hand.) It is best illustrated by our old friend Basil Brush. Two people are required. One is hidden below the pulpit, or whatever

Figure 5

is being used, and he manipulates the doll and provides the voice. The other, with whom the doll engages in conversation, is in full view. The one below can have a script, thus enabling the conversation to be followed accurately as it has been worked out. For this you must have a puppet with mouth movements: probably an animal glove puppet is best.

There is, however, a great deal to be said for a full ventriloquil dialogue using a professionally made boy or girl Vent doll. Very quickly the doll becomes a personality and everybody knows him/her by name. The great advantage of this method is that everybody can see and hear what is going on as clearly as they can see and hear the preacher. The congregation become very much part of the dialogue because questions are asked and answered which they would like to ask and have answered. This means of communication is not only fascinating to both children and adults, but it also captivates the congregation. They listen, usually with rapt attention. It is also quite often the best way of saying something within a live situation. The congregation see themselves in the Vent doll. It must, however, be done well, and this means learning the skills of ventriloquism, which takes time.

I have used a boy and girl puppet together. For this rather more complicated usage, one of the dolls needs to be adapted for the left hand. Eg, eyes that move to the right rather than the left. Left-handed presenters must watch out for this when ordering or selecting a doll.

## Rules for presentation

1 The script must be very carefully worked out. Some people are gifted in this field—try out your Christian school teachers. The language of a local boy or girl aged nine to twelve years is about right.
2 Never make your Vent doll do anything a normal human wouldn't do, eg, twist its head right round or sit on your knee. Your doll needs to have a personality of its own.
3 Don't go on longer than ten minutes, otherwise you will lose your voice and your congregation.
4 Bring your doll on as naturally as you can. My two dolls, Jerry and Sue, are produced from behind a model brick wall or by letting up the blind in the window of a model house. Never bring them out of a case or leave them, at the end of a talk, lolling motionless on a chair.
5 Use a neck microphone rather than one on a stand. It leaves you less restricted.
6 Ring the changes. Don't use puppets every week, or even every month, but advertise well when you do. A series of three is usually long enough.

7 Never use your doll for secular purposes. It damages the image.

## How do I begin?

Ventriloquil techniques are improving all the time and good self-taught ventriloquists are few and far between. Get a book and study it. *Ventriloquism for Beginners* by Douglas Houlden is a good starter. This book sets out a basic technique and gives many useful hints in presentation.

Good Vent dolls are, however, very difficult to come by. An advert in a theatrical paper, eg, *Stage Door*, will often bring a response. Do get a good model, preferably one which doesn't have a chin which falls away from the face, because they never look real.

The cost may be between £25 and £100. New dolls can be obtained from L. Davenport and Co., 51 Great Russell Street, London WC1. But be prepared to wait up to six months and pay as much as £150 for a top professional model. They can also supply excellent animal puppets from time to time. They sometimes have secondhand puppets for sale.

The best selection of string puppets in this country is obtainable from Pelham Puppets, Marlborough, Wilts. If you purchased one of their top marionettes, you could probably use it as a model for making your own. Glove and stick puppets are easily made. *Let's make puppets* by E. G. Vince, available from Church Information Office, Church House, Westminster, London SW1, is a good buy.

Before launching out in any direction in puppetry, reconcile yourself to the fact that it will take quite a lot of time, but if well done it brings its rewards. Seek the help of someone who has already used this method of communication, and take every opportunity of watching any form of puppetry on TV. If it impresses you with its potential for conveying the Gospel, you will almost certainly impress others once you have acquired the skills.

*Donald Churchman*

# PART ONE

## *Talks and Drama*

# 1 Jesus Christ: His Incarnation

## TEXT

Philippians 2:5–11.

## AIM

To present the true meaning of the Christmas story very vividly.

## PREPARATION

Dress up in some very old and dirty clothes, but on top of these wear your normal surplice, cassock, etc. Have concealed near the pulpit an old hat and also a dustbin with a cross in it made out of red paper that can easily be pulled out and hung over the dustbin. Write in large letters on the cross itself 'He carried our sins', as illustrated in Figure 8. Also have ready at the chancel steps (but out of sight) robes to represent the dress of a king. These should include a crown and a garment that will completely cover the dustman's clothes. The crown can be made out of cardboard and painted gold.

Before the service begins give a number of people in the congregation some pieces of paper with various sins marked on them, such as Greed, Lying, Lust, Hate, etc.

Figure 6

## PRESENTATION

Immediately after the congregation are seated, read out in a very solemn voice texts from the Bible that speak of the holiness and majesty of God, such as Isaiah 6:3; 40:12, 15, 17, 22–23, 25–36; Habakkuk 1:3. After reading these words relax your voice and say, 'If God is so pure and holy, and he is, how can you and I escape the judgement and penalty that we deserve for our sins?' Go on to explain that God is also loving, quoting John 3:16. Refer to Philippians 2 and as you read verses 5–7 gradually remove all your church robes, step down from the pulpit, put on the old hat, pick up the dustbin and start walking down the nave asking people if they have any sins to declare. As these are produced, comment appropriately on each sin so that it obviously applies to members of the congregation. End each comment with 'God must judge those who are greedy (lie, hate, etc)' and put the sins in the dustbin in such a way that some can still be seen hanging over the side.

Figure 7

When you have collected up all the sins, make your way to the back of the church. Push all the sins right into the dustbin and pull out the cross. Walk back up the aisle with the cross showing and continue to quote from Philippians 2:9–11.

Figure 8

On reaching the chancel steps place your dustbin down and dress up in the robes of a king. Conclude by pointing out that this is what Jesus has done for you. He came down to earth at the first Christmas to die for your sins, which he did on the first Good Friday. But God raised him from the dead and exalted him to the place of greatest honour in heaven. We need to accept him as our saviour from sin and give him the place of honour in our lives as our rightful king.

*Michael Botting*

# 2 The Man with Four Friends

## TEXT

Mark 2:1–12.

## AIM

To apply the lessons from one of Jesus' healing miracles.

## PREPARATION

Prepare three cards with the words 'forgiveness', 'friendship' and 'faith' on them. After the sketch is over the cards can be put on a visual-aid board at the appropriate time or held by three members of the cast.

## SKETCH

*Cast:* Four male disciples, three female friends, one male friend who is also brother of one of the ladies.
*Costume:* Traditional first-century Palestinian dress.
*Props:* Three low seats for the ladies.

## PRESENTATION

As soon as the congregation are seated following the hymn before the talk, switch on the stage lights as a cue for the playlet to begin. Immediately the sketch ends switch off the stage lights and switch on the visual-aid board spotlight.

Three women, each occupied in some way, are seated on the stage (red and white stage lights give an attractive effect).

SALOME: They are an awful long time. Do you think something's wrong?

RACHEL: They have probably got caught in the crowds. This new teacher, Jesus, from Nazareth, is terribly popular, and with his healing powers, thousands—literally thousands—are crowding around him wherever he goes.

MARY: Besides, it is quite a long trek from Capernaum carrying Simon, even though there are four of them.

SALOME: Oh I do hope Jesus has been able to do something. Simon has really set his heart on this. He will be so disappointed.

MARY: How long has he been like that, Salome?

SALOME: He has been a paralytic for as long as I can remember.

RACHEL: It must have been a terrible strain—

(Five men burst in from the front of the stage with Simon, carrying a bed rolled up under his arm, running in first. Before he reaches the stage he begins shouting.)

SIMON: Salome, I am cured, I am cured! Praise be to God! Your prayers have been answered. John, James, Peter and Thomas were marvellous.

(He throws his arms around his sister, Salome.)

MARY: Praise the Lord! But what happened?

JOHN: We got to the house where the Teacher was and it was swamped. The crowds were impossible. It was very much worse than at the games, or even at the Roman arena, I'd swear.

SIMON: The lads were tremendous. Never say die. They knew it was impossible to get near Jesus in any normal way so what do you think they did?

SALOME: Go on.

RACHEL: I can't wait to hear.

PETER: We managed at last to get through the crowds to the steps up on to the flat roof. From there we were able to get just over where we thought the Master was in the room below. Then Thomas—

THOMAS: I managed to make an opening in the roof. Meanwhile James found some ropes and, tying these to the four corners of the bed, we—

SALOME: You lowered him down.

RACHEL: Oh you boys. You really are clever. Then what happened?

JAMES: The crowd in the house was astonished, as you can imagine, but the Teacher was wonderful. He stood there so dignified and yet so understanding. There was a lovely smile on his face.

JOHN: I thought I heard him mutter, 'What faith! What faith!'

PETER: And then he said a most astonishing thing. It really shocked the scribes that were sitting there.

SIMON: He said to me, 'My son, your sins are forgiven.'

THOMAS: The scribes started shouting 'Blasphemy' and asking 'Who can forgive sins but God?'

JAMES: But he was more than equal to them. He obviously knew what they were thinking. He stood erect and said to them very directly, and loud enough for us to hear, 'Why do you question this in your heart? Which is easier, to say, "Your sins are forgiven," or to say, "Rise, take up your pallet and walk"?'

JOHN: He had a point there. Anyone can say, 'Your sins are forgiven,' but who can cure a paralytic? Surely a man who can cure a paralytic perhaps has a right to say, 'Your sins are forgiven.'

JAMES: Jesus then said to the scribes, 'But that you may know that the Son of Man has authority on earth to forgive sins....'

SIMON: Then he said to me, 'I say to you, rise, take up your pallet, and go home.' Immediately he said it I felt all warm inside. My whole body tingled. I just suddenly knew I could stand up and walk—and I did! Oh, praise the Lord! I believe that man could be the Messiah.

JOHN: Everyone was saying things like that. The whole crowd was praising God as it made a way for us to come home.

What did the man want from Jesus? What did he get first? (Place 'forgiveness' on the visual-aid board.) Why? Enlarge on our need for forgiveness. How did the man know he was forgiven? (See verses 10–12.) How did he ever get this forgiveness? Ultimately because Jesus was to die for his sins. But that was only part of the story. What else had to happen? He was offered 'friendship' (put word on board). It was because of the man's friends that he was taken to Jesus to be cured. However, there was something else (see verse 5): 'faith' (put word on board). It was because of the men's faith that Jesus was able to cure him of his physical and spiritual troubles.

*Michael Botting*

# 3 The Pharisee and the Tax Man

## TEXT

Luke 18:9–14

## AIM

To apply one of Jesus' parables by means of a mime and pre-recorded script.

## PREPARATION

Prerecord the script included in the Presentation. The words in brackets at the end of the preacher's script could gradually fade out. Arrange to have a curate or someone dressed up to look like a clergyman in the pulpit, well lit up, say by means of the light over the pulpit reading desk. On a stage on the other side of the chancel have a small congregation with two men particularly prominent who can be lit up with red (Pharisee) and green (Publican) lights, according to when they are thinking aloud.

## PRESENTATION

VICAR (unrecorded): What is about to happen at this moment in your pew, where *you* are sitting? You may decide to 'switch off'. Or you may think to yourself in different ways about what is being said in this talk.

We are now going to look in and listen in on the Sunday worship at St Isosceles and All Angles (*enter preacher and congregation*) to hear not only what the preacher is preaching but also what two members of his congregation are thinking and praying.

The sermon has already started—the preacher has been talking about the first of the Ten Commandments, 'Thou shall have no other gods before me'. He has just reached his third point.

*Recording:*

PREACHER: ...first then we must *know* about God, secondly we must *believe* in God, and thirdly we must *confess* God. We have to make it known publicly and openly that this God, who is the Creator of the world, and who sent Jesus Christ, is our God and we have no other.

A young man may have a girlfriend. He has got to know her very well, to him she is the only girl in the world, and everyone else knows that he thinks that way about her. One day they are going to get married, but they cannot do so secretly—everyone will have to know. The wedding must be public and they will both want it that way.

In the same way we must make it obvious that we worship the one true God—we must confess him. How do we do this? We acknowledge him publicly, say by coming to church. Why do you come to church?

PHARISEE: Well he doesn't need to tell me that—I've been coming all these years. Well I mean to say, it's my duty. Look at Mrs Roper. She hasn't been for weeks. She only comes when it suits her, and then only to show off her new hat. Not like me. Here every week without fail, that's me. O yes, God, you can rely on me.

PUBLICAN: I've never really thought about why I come to church—s'ppose I've just got into the habit of coming. Anyway, all my friends are here—I'm sure it's the right thing—besides I need the help to find out how to stop doing some of the things I do that make me feel—so bad.

PREACHER: Then we must *love* God. He must have first place in our lives. What has the first place in your life? Money, the TV, your record collection, clothes? How much more important is it to you to spend time with them rather than God? Are you really putting God first in your life? Or is it the telly or car?

PHARISEE: Putting God first? Well honestly! I ask you. Of course I am. And every day at that. Sunday there's morning and evening service. Monday is youth club night. Tuesday is visiting night. I could go on and on. Loving God is surely loving other people. And what I am doing, day in and day out at that. You know I love you God and I put you first in everything I do—much more than some I know!

PUBLICAN: Lord, you seem to have the last place in my life—I just don't seem to have time to do half the things some people here do—by the time I've finished my homework and given Mum a hand. S'ppose I do watch the telly quite a bit—lot of rubbish some of it.

PREACHER: Putting God first means really trusting him. It means putting your life completely in his hands. It means saying, 'Lord, you run my life.' Do you really trust him? (I wonder if you have heard this story.)

PHARISEE: And trust him? Really, what a question to ask! While others fall by the wayside I soldier on under the banner of Christ. I know he is with me. I wouldn't be on so many committees if he wasn't, would I now? And at work, well everyone knows what I believe—I make sure of that! God knows I trust him and he knows he can trust me. Where would this church be...

PUBLICAN: I know the Bible says, 'Do not be anxious about your life' and worrying won't help—or something like that, but I find it so difficult to trust you blindly for my future. I do wish you would send me some definite advice sometimes.

PREACHER: In closing, let me say that to put your life entirely in God's hands is not easy. I know it's difficult and most important; God understands our weakness. He knows that we often fail him, and yet the wonderful thing is that he still loves us. (Let us bow our heads for prayer.)

PHARISEE: God, I thank you that I am just not like other people. You have raised me to be a cut above the rest and this can only be due to my unfailing loyalty and devotion to your service. I will continue coming to church every Sunday and will continue to carry out all my good works in the parish during the week. I thank you that I can give up the time, not like other people who think far more of themselves and would never think of doing that something extra for you. I do more than enough. I come to church at least twice a week, and donate a regular amount to the church and charity every week. I thank you God that you have made me as I am.

PUBLICAN: Lord, you've really shown me what I'm like inside. How I've been crowding you out of my life. I can only thank you that you love me so much, in spite of my many failings. Forgive me, Lord, and help me to make this week different. Amen.

Conclude the talk as follows:

Let's think about the first man whose thoughts we overheard. He was a religious man like the Pharisees who were Jewish leaders during Jesus' time on earth. Was he really praying? No, he did not need to pray. He did not think there was anything wrong with him. He just talked to himself about how good he was and, as Jesus said, 'They that are whole have no need of a physician.'

What about the other man? He was rather like some publicans or tax collectors in the New Testament, such as Zacchaeus or Matthew. He knew God was holy, that he himself was a sinner and needed forgiveness. We know from the story on which ours today was based that he could leave church forgiven, unlike the other man. Who are you most like? Will you leave this church today knowing you are forgiven?

*Michael Botting*

# 4 Masks

TEXT

John 8:31–3.

AIM

To show how, although we use masks to hide behind, Jesus accepts us just as we are, shows us the truth about ourselves, and sets us free in his love.

PREPARATION

Obtain a mask, eg, animal, clown, etc. Rehearse the role-play, requiring two to eight people.

PRESENTATION

(1) Put on the mask and pretend to be whatever the mask represents. Ask if any one really believes that you have become what the mask depicts.

(2) Remove the mask and then talk about how many people wear 'masks'—they pretend to be what they are not. For example, some boys pretend to be macho when inside they are frightened, and some girls pretend to be street-wise when they are just showing off.

(3) In the church people can wear 'masks' too. Here are some of them: (encourage people to laugh at the role-play).

*I'm good*

I've never done anyone any harm. I lead a good life. I don't smoke or drink. I'm good to my family. I work hard at my job. I even go to church on Sunday. I'm a thoroughly *good* person!

*I'm no good*

Don't ask me to get involved in anything. I'd make a mess of even the simplest thing. I'm a complete failure. I don't know why anyone bothers with me. I'm such a weakling, don't expect *anything* of me, but make sure you look after *me*!

*I'm jolly*

I'm always smiling, always good for a laugh, a joke at the ready whatever the situation. *No one's* allowed to be miserable if I'm around. I'm the life and soul of every party. *No one* has a get-together without asking me to come. They really *need* my humour.

*I'm shy*

I'm too shy to say a word. I'll get embarrassed. Everyone thinks I'm stupid. I've nothing to say, I couldn't say it if I had. Anyway, I'd *rather* stay in my shell—it's much safer!

*I'm religious*

I go to all the mid-week services and twice on Sundays. I never miss. I'm a key member of the prayer group, the missionary committee and my house group, and I spend whole days in prayer and fasting. I have such a blessed life. I feel sorry for those *less dedicated* than me!

*I'm ill*

I'd really like to help but I have to be very careful. It's my heart, it flutters. I'm on three sorts of tablets and my doctor is *very* worried about me. I could go at any time. I need looking after myself, so don't ask *anything* of me!

*I'm rebellious*

I'm really into drink and drugs. I get high every weekend and stay out all night. The girls think I'm fantastic. I follow all the fashions, I'm the first to get the latest gear. I like to shock my parents, in fact I'll do anything if it's *opposite* to their views!

*I'm busy*

I'm president of the Mother's Union and PCC secretary. I'm always out helping others. Monday it's Play Group, Tuesday, the Pensioners' club. Wednesdays I'm with 'Meals on Wheels'.

Thursday, the Mothers' Union and Fridays, it's hospital visiting. I *never* stop. I just don't know how people would cope *without me*!

Do you recognise any one? Do you recognise yourself? It's not that it's wrong to help other people or to be ill or shy or even rebellious, but it is wrong when we pretend, by wearing 'a mask' which hides the real person, so that we avoid facing the truth about ourselves.

(4) Why do people wear masks? Get answers from the congregation. (Likely answers will be—out of fear; as a defence to protect us from hurt and rejection; because we think people won't like us if we let them see what we're really like.)

(5) Did Jesus ever wear a mask? No, he was free to be himself. Jesus loves each of us, just as we are, and longs for us to be free to love him, not to hide behind a mask. If we let him remove our mask, he is able to change us from the inside and set us free from the fears that made us wear that mask in the first place.

*Margi Walker*

# 5 Giving

## TEXT

2 Corinthians 9:7.

## AIM

To teach Christian giving and how we can become cheerful givers.

## PREPARATION

*Introduction:* A small globe of the world, a cross, a Bible, (obtain or make up) an old-fashioned pair of scales, a picture of a heart. Part 1: An old-fashioned money purse around your belt and a brass bowl. Part 2: A small offertory plate or bag, together with drama items: item of food, clothing, car, house, and pocket money. Part 3: Large offertory plate and plenty of miscellaneous items from the playgroup toybox. Part 4: Large offertory plate.

## PRESENTATION

(Note: Each section could be amplified into a full sermon, or a short teaching series.)

### *Introduction*

God has given us so much, but how much do we give back to him? God the Father made the world and us, and he gave us the world. God the Son died for our sins. God the Holy Spirit helps us in so many ways. Let me illustrate this with these old-fashioned scales. On one side I put God's world, the cross and the Bible. What can we put on our side to balance this out? Can we ever give enough back to God to thank him for everything? On the other side put a picture of the heart or ourselves to weigh down the scales. We can never pay God enough in return, but simply offer him our lives.

*(1) Secret* (Yourself and someone else in dramatic presentation).

Jesus taught, in Matthew 6, about 'when' we give, not 'if'. He said that our left hand must not know what our right hand is doing. What does this mean? Imagine the scene in a busy market area of Jerusalem. A Jewish Pharisee with his money bag comes across a beggar. In order to show off to the greatest extent he calls out, 'Stand back, I am going to give this beggar some money. I'll give the first coin that comes out of my purse.' (The crowd wonders how much that will be—the equivalent of a penny, a pound or something like £50). The beggar holds up the brass bowl (get someone from the congregation to do this for you). The Pharisee holds his money bag in his left hand while his right hand stretches into it and fumbles around trying to feel the different sizes of coins (describe this process). He tries to weigh up with his mind what coins his right hand can pick to try to give the appearance of generosity, while his left hand, testing the weight of the bag, wants to feel how much money is left after the coin is given. The left hand was certainly wanting to know what the right hand was doing before the decision was made. He then pulls out a coin and tosses it over to the beggar's brass bowl (demonstrate this). It makes a loud ringing sound for all to hear. How proud he must feel. Jesus said, 'You must not be like this.' (Perhaps go on to discuss how people give at church.)

*(2) Systematic*

Paul taught, in 1 Corinthians 16, that we need to organise our giving so that other people do not need to know about it. (Perhaps describe what happens in your church here), and show the normal offertory plate or bag.) Get six people to come to the front in turn and say (into the microphone), 'Spend money on me. I am food' (holding aloft a food item, eg, a cornflakes packet). Also: 'I am clothing / the car / the mortgage, rent, insurance / the heating bills / pocket money'. Finally, quietly holding offertory bag: 'Please remember me: I am doing God's work.' Each one keeps shouting, except the last, until the preacher shouts, 'Order! Be quiet. I can't cope with all this shouting and competition. I need to get you organised. Get into a line. (They push around into a line, jostling for places.) The preacher then says to the one with the offertory bag, 'Now you had the quiet calm voice, so I will put you at the front and give my money to you first. Then the others will all be in second place, and we will each have our own order for them.

*(3) Spontaneous*

King David once made an appeal and found that so much had been given that even the huge collection plate was not big enough to hold it all. They had to ask the people to stop giving (1 Chron 29)! First give miscellaneous toys out to children and others as they arrive in church. It may be wise for the person handing out the toys to say they have to be handed over during the service, in case there are any reluctant givers! To try to illustrate this, let me ask our treasurer to take up the offertory of all those toys we gave out at the beginning of the service. As the plate comes near you, pile on as many toys as you can. This carries on until no more can be added, and you have to ask people to stop giving.

*(4) Sacrificial*

This is based on a true story. (It can be acted out by using a very large offertory plate and a small child.) In an old chapel long ago there was a challenging talk about mission. The congregation consisted largely of rich people. There was an appeal for a collection for the needy missionaries. The sidesman passed the collection plate round from the back of the church to the front. Now at the front of the church was a very poor widow with her crippled child. As the plate moved through the pews from the back towards the front of the church, people wondered if he would even bother to pass the plate to this poor woman and her child. The sidesman got near the front and paused for a moment in hesitation: was he to embarrass the widow and the child, or pass them by which could be even worse? The crippled boy took the initiative and said, 'Please sir, put the plate on the floor.' The boy left his seat, wriggled over the floor and sat himself on the plate, 'Please sir, I'm ready now.' The truth slowly dawned on the sidesman and bit by bit it dawned on the rest of the congregation. The sidesman lifted up the plate with the boy and brought it to the front. The boy had given everything he had. There were tears in many eyes as that offertory was dedicated to the service of God.

*Conclusion:* Summary and challenge.

*David Williams*

# PART TWO

## *Dialogues for Use with Puppets*

# 6 Do You Believe in Father Christmas?

## TEXT

2 Corinthians 9:15.

## AIM

To remind us of God's wonderful gift to us.

## PRESENTATION

Jerry is dressed in casual clothes. It is Christmas time so he has a number of presents with him.

DON: Hello Jerry, I see you're getting ready for Christmas.
JERRY: You bet! I love Christmas!
DON: I'm sure you do. I expect you're looking forward to having a visit from Father Christmas.
JERRY: You must be joking!
DON: What do you mean—joking?
JERRY: You don't really think I believe all that kid's stuff do you?
DON: What kid's stuff?
JERRY: Well, Father Christmas and all that rubbish.
DON: Rubbish? It's not rubbish at all!
JERRY: 'Course it is—it's a lot of silly nonsense. Father Christmas, indeed!
DON: Are you trying to tell me, Jerry, you don't believe in Father Christmas?
JERRY: Of course I don't, and neither do you.
DON: But I do.
JERRY: [*Incredulously*] You don't!
DON: Yes, I do.
JERRY: [*questioningly*] You do?
DON: Yes, I really do.
JERRY: [*even more incredulously*] You don't. You're winding me up.
DON: Jerry, I honestly believe in Father Christmas.
JERRY: Didn't your mother ever tell you?

DON: Tell me what?

JERRY: [*Aside*] Do you know, everybody, I don't think he's ever been told.
[*To Don*] You must be mad.

DON: Mad?

JERRY: Yes, crazy. So you really believe in Father Christmas?

DON: Yes, I do.

JERRY: Riding over the clouds in a sleigh?

DON: I didn't say that, did I?

JERRY: No, but that's what Father Christmas does, isn't it?

DON: It may be what the fairy story Father Christmas does, but not the real one.

JERRY: What do you mean, the fairy story Father Christmas?

DON: Well, take the story of George and the Dragon. Now there really was a St George, but a lot of legends have grown up round him and rather fanciful stories written. The things described in the legends and stories didn't really happen, they're just fairy stories using St George as the make-believe hero.

JERRY: What's that got to do with Father Christmas?

DON: Well, there really was a Father Christmas once.

JERRY: I don't believe it.

DON: All right, give me another name for Father Christmas.

JERRY: Old Red-nose.

DON: Now come on, be sensible.

JERRY: OK, what about Santa Claus?

DON: Very good, but where do you think he got that strange name from?

JERRY: I don't know, but you're going to tell me aren't you?

DON: If you like. It comes from St Nicholas, or as they pronounce it where he came from, St Nichlaus. If you repeat that quickly it soon sounds like Santa Claus, doesn't it?

JERRY: You mean to tell me that Father Christmas was a saint?

DON: He certainly was. Would you like me to tell you about him?

JERRY: Yes, go ahead.

DON: St Nicholas was a very good bishop who lived near Freiburg in a mountainous part of Germany. He noticed that at Christmas time, with all the festivities going on, the people forgot all about God. Especially the wealthy ones.

JERRY: Go on.

DON: He also noticed that the very poor people who were cold and hungry were miserable and thought God had forgotten all about them.

JERRY: What did he do?

DON: He thought of a way of encouraging those who had plenty to help those who had very little.

JERRY: How did he do that?

DON: Well, he called on the rich people and told them about the poor people, and because they liked the kind bishop they were ready to do something about it, and gave him gifts for the poor people.

JERRY: [*enthusiastically*] Don't keep stopping, tell me more.

DON: St Nicholas gathered all the goodies he'd been given, disguised himself with a cloak and at Christmas time he left parcels of clothes, food and money outside their homes.

JERRY: But why Christmas time?

DON: For two reasons. First because winter was coming on, and when the snow came the people began to feel the cold and food was scarce.

JERRY: What was the other reason?

DON: Because he wanted the people to remember that God also gave a wonderful present to the world when it was in need, and he thought this was a good way to remind them.

JERRY: Why did he disguise himself?

DON: Because he wanted the people to say thank you to God and not to him, and to remember that *all* good things come from God.

JERRY: Did they ever find out who'd been doing it?

DON: Yes, they did in time, and for years (even today) when a boy or a girl received a surprise present they used to say, 'the good St Nicholas must have left it.'

JERRY: So this idea of giving presents at Christmas time is to remind us of the gift God gave us.

DON: That's right, and here's a way of remembering something about that wonderful gift, so sit back and watch: (Here introduce a simple board on which the four letters GIFT can be placed easily, with the left hand for Jerry and everyone to see.)

| | |
|---|---|
| G stands for *God* | Use the word Emmanuel—God with us. |
| I stands for *Inside* | He came to share his life—I will never leave you, etc. |
| F stands for *Free* | We don't have to earn this gift. |
| T stands for *Trust* | He will never fail us in any of his promises. Won't let us down. |

JERRY: Do you know, I think I believe in Father Christmas after all, but in a new way.

DON: Well done Jerry, I hope everyone here does as well. Happy Christmas to you all.

# 7 Motives

## TEXT

1 Samuel 16:7.

## AIM

To consider our motives for doing things.

## PRESENTATION

Jerry is wearing choir robes.

| | |
|---|---|
| DON: | And why, may I ask, are you wearing choir robes, Jerry? |
| JERRY: | I'm going to join the church choir. |
| DON: | I suppose you realise that before joining the choir you have to have a voice test, and after that, an interview with me. |
| JERRY: | Oh dear! I didn't think I'd have to go through all that. |
| DON: | Well there's no time like the present, and seeing you are all dressed in choir robes we might as well have the voice test straight away. |
| JERRY: | I...I can't sing without any music. |
| DON: | If you can sing at all, Jerry, you'll be able to manage all right. |
| JERRY: | [*aside*] I don't think I'm going to like this. |
| DON: | [*aside*] I don't think I am either, but we have to go through with it. Ah! Here's Mr Arneill [the organist] he'll be able to give us some music. |
| MR ARNEILL: | Good morning, Vicar, I see we have a new recruit. Well I never! If it isn't Jerry. |
| JERRY: | [*aside*] Oh no, this is going to be dreadful. |
| DON: | Yes Mr Arneill, and Jerry has very kindly consented to having a voice test straight away. I wonder whether you would be good enough to accompany him on the piano. Just play the tune through quietly and then Jerry can sing |

us a verse. The first verse of 'Abide with me'.

*[Jerry looks very flustered and then sings one verse of 'Abide with me'. Expressions of horror on the faces of Mr Arneill and Don.]*

JERRY: [*Before the last echo has died down.*] How's that?

MR ARNEILL: [*Collecting his manuscript.*] I don't think you'll be needing me any further, Vicar. Good morning.

DON: I'm afraid, Jerry, Mr Arneill has made it quite clear that you haven't quite got the quality of voice he's looking for.

JERRY: I haven't! [*Incredulously.*] Well, who gave me my voice anyway?

DON: Well, I suppose the answer to that one must be God.

JERRY: Then why should God give me a voice that's no good?

DON: Look at it like this, Jerry. It's quite true that God gave you a voice, but then God gave voices to crows as well as canaries, and crows' voices weren't made for singing. They have different ways of expressing their talents.

JERRY: Are you telling me I sing like a crow?

DON: No, I'm simply saying we all have different gifts, and I'm quite sure in your heart of hearts you know very well that singing doesn't happen to be one of yours. Now tell me, why do you really want to join the choir?

JERRY: [*After a pause.*] For the lolly.

DON: I see, you just wanted to earn some spending money, and thought this was as good a way of doing it as any.

JERRY: Is that wrong?

DON: No, it certainly isn't wrong to want to earn some money, but there are higher motives and nobler reasons for joining a church choir, Jerry, than just to earn some money.

JERRY: Such as?

DON: Wanting to serve God, for one thing, and trying to help others to worship him for another.

JERRY: My friend Sidney's in the choir, and I know he's there just for the money.

DON: We mustn't judge other people, Jerry, we have to make sure that right motives govern everything *we* do.

JERRY: Everything?

DON: Yes, everything.

JERRY: I don't quite understand.

DON: Well, it's like this. Do you remember that Sunday School outing when Sidney pushed his sister into the duck pond, and you very gallantly jumped in and pulled her out?

JERRY: Cor yes! I remember that well.

DON: And do you remember what a hero you were and how everyone said you were the bravest boy in the town?

JERRY: [*Smiling all over his face.*] I certainly do.

DON: And how your headmaster made special mention of you at school assembly the following Monday morning?

JERRY: You can say that again, I thought I might even get knighted.

DON: And how in the newspaper you were reported as saying that you would have done it for anyone?

JERRY: Did I say that?

DON: You did. Well now Jerry, as we are on our own, perhaps you would like to tell me the real reason for jumping in the water and pulling poor Sue out.

JERRY: To tell the truth, it was because she had my stick of rock in her pocket.

DON: That's what I mean, Jerry. You weren't really a hero at all. You were just being selfish, thinking of yourself and that stick of rock.

JERRY: You do make me feel rotten.

DON: Always remember, every Christian action must be done with the highest motive and for the very best reason—namely to please and serve God. Now off you go, and hang those choir robes up neatly in the vestry. You won't be needing them for a while.
[*Turning to congregation.*] Do you remember the

words the Lord said to Samuel? 'Man looks on the outward appearance, but God looks on the heart.'

# 8 Transformed

TEXT

John 3:3.

AIM

That like Nicodemus we must all be born spiritually.

PRESENTATION

Jerry has with him a shoe-box with holes in the lid.

DON: Hello Jerry, what have we here?
JERRY: Just a shoe-box.
DON: What's the idea of all these little holes? To let the smell out?
JERRY: Oh no. I don't think you'll guess what I've got in here.
DON: Is it animal, vegetable or mineral?
JERRY: Well, I suppose it's animal with vegetable connections.
DON: Animal with vegetable connections! It sounds like a guinea pig with a cauliflower ear to me.
JERRY: No, it's nothing like that.
DON: Is it dead or alive?
JERRY: Very much alive; at least I think they are. They were this morning.
DON: Can you give me a clue?
JERRY: Well here's a riddle. Can you tell me what it is that goes 99 clonk, 99 clonk, 99 clonk?
DON: 99 Clonk? I give up.
JERRY: A centipede with a wooden leg.
DON: Oh Jerry, you're not collecting centipedes now are you?
JERRY: Take the lid off and have a look.
DON: [*Removes lid.*] I can't see anything but lettuce leaves.
JERRY: They're underneath—my caterpillars, can't you see them? Actually they're silk worms, and I'm not quite sure where to hide them.
DON: Why do you have to hide them?

JERRY: I used to keep them on the shelf in the kitchen, but yesterday I left the lid off by mistake and at tea-time Dad found two of them in his salad. And he said he wasn't going to allow them to stay in the house a day longer.

DON: You should have explained to him what a good thing it was that he found them. Supposing he had finished his salad without finding them? I don't know what to suggest.

JERRY: Do you think I could hide them under my bed?

DON: You could try it, as long as they don't keep you awake at night with their chewing. [*Looking into box again.*] I shouldn't think it would be long before they start spinning their cocoons. I could use a nice new silk tie. Do you think they could manage it?

JERRY: No, I don't keep them for the silk. I just like to see them turn into chrysalises and then into moths. Some of the Indian silk moths are huge, and you should see the colours.

DON: I'd certainly like to see them, Jerry. It really is amazing how these ugly-looking caterpillars can change into such lovely moths.

JERRY: Wouldn't it be exciting if we could do the same. Have a huge meal, then a long sleep, and then after a lovely dream suddenly find you're quite different.

DON: You know Jerry, there's a very long word which describes this wonderful change caterpillars go through—it's the word 'metamorphosis'; it means a change in outward appearance.

JERRY: It can't happen to us, can it?

DON: Strange as it may sound, Jerry, this very word is used in the Bible to explain how people can be born again into a new kind of life.

JERRY: Do you mean when we die?

DON: No, this is something that happens when a person becomes a Christian. He receives a new kind of life from God, and if this new birth is real then there is the outward change and we become more and more like the Lord Jesus Christ himself.

JERRY: I wish that would happen to my teacher at school, she's a real...

DON: Now Jerry, that'll do. This is something that has to begin in each one of us. If we become different then perhaps other people will become different too. Now you run along and make sure those caterpillars don't get into your father's salad again. Cheerio.

Between you, me and the gatepost, have you ever stopped to consider what Jesus meant when he said to Nicodemus, 'You must be born again'? You can read it in St John's Gospel, chapter 3. Goodbye.

# 9 Play the Game

## TEXT

Exodus 20:1–17; Matthew 22:35–40.

## AIM

To show that we must have rules for life.

## PRESENTATION

Jerry is wearing a school blazer, rosette, woolly hat and scarf in a well-known football team colours.

DON: Well look who's coming, it's World Cup Willie himself. Well Jerry, how did the game go this afternoon?
JERRY: It was a great match—and our side got the only goal in the game.
DON: What, only one goal?
JERRY: Yes, but that was enough.
DON: That's odd! When I used to play every game had two goals, one at each end.
JERRY: [*Sarcastically.*] Ha! Ha! Ha! Very funny. Things are quite different now you know, not like they used to be in the olden days.
DON: What do you mean, 'olden days'!
JERRY: Well, for instance, they wear proper shorts now. In your day their trousers went down below their knees.
DON: Now then, I don't want any cheek from you, my lad. I'll have you know I used to play Right Back for my school team.
JERRY: [*Aside*] Right back in the dressing-room I should think.
DON: I beg your pardon.
JERRY: Oh nothing. I just said the team were glad to get back in the dressing-room.
DON: Why was that?
JERRY: It was raining cats and dogs.
DON: And I suppose the pitch was covered in poodles.
JERRY: On form today, aren't we?

DON: Well, all joking apart, was it a good game?

JERRY: Not really. Too many fouls and late tackles. Do you know, one tackle was so late I think it must have been left over from the last match.

DON: That doesn't sound very nice.

JERRY: And I'll tell you something else; I'm going to sock Sidney one on the nose at school on Monday.

DON: Whatever for?

JERRY: Because he cheered when one of our lads got kicked on the ankle.

DON: Punching someone on the nose on Monday for something that happened on Saturday seems like another very late tackle to me.

JERRY: He deserves it.

DON: It seems to me, Jerry, that it was a bit of a rough game with nobody bothering very much about the rules. Now I've got an idea for getting rid of all fouls in football matches.

JERRY: Really? That sounds like a good idea.

DON: Yes! Why not do away with rules altogether, then nobody can break them anymore.

JERRY: You can't do that. How can you have a real game without rules?

DON: You think we must have rules then?

JERRY: Of course you must. You know what people are like—take away the rules and all the little guys like me would get kicked around by the big ones, and nobody could stop them. You've just got to have rules.

DON: All right Jerry, I see your point. But surely, if we need to have rules for our games, don't you think we also need to have rules for our lives?

JERRY: Yes, I suppose we do. After all, if everybody goes around doing just what they like, a lot of people are going to get hurt, aren't they?

DON: They certainly are, and I think this is one reason why God gave us rules for our lives.

JERRY: Do you mean the Ten Commandments?

DON: Yes, the ones God gave to Moses that we find written in the Bible.

JERRY: Are they the only rules God gave?

DON: Oh no, there are many more. But Jesus said we would

be keeping every rule God gave if we were to love God with all our heart and strength and mind, and love other people as much as we love ourselves.

JERRY: That isn't easy, is it?

DON: No, it isn't. But then it isn't always easy to keep the rules in football, especially if someone trips us up purposely. But for the sake of the game, a good footballer keeps to the rules and in consequence enjoys the game much better.

JERRY: You know something, I don't think I'll sock Sidney on the nose after all.

DON: Glad to hear it Jerry. You'll certainly play a better game in life if you keep that spirit up. Well, off you go and I hope you'll have a better match next week.

Between you, me and the gatepost, a lot of people think God's rules for life are a bore, but when you stop to consider what life would be like if we took them away, you begin to realise just how important it is to have them. Goodbye.

# 10 Friends of God

## TEXT

Proverbs 18:24.

## AIM

To show the importance of forgiveness.

## PRESENTATION

Jerry appears with an eye-shade and his arm in a sling.

DON: Jerry, whatever's happened? You look as if you've been to the wars.

JERRY: If you really want to know, I fell out with Sidney.

DON: What did you fall out of, a sky-scraper?

JERRY: We didn't fall out of anything, we just fell out with each other. We had a quarrel on the way home from school.

DON: Oh, I see what you mean, you've been fighting again. You ought to know better, especially as you always seem to get the worst of it. Well what was the trouble about this time?

JERRY: He said his football team were going to get the Cup this year, and I said that the only cup they would get would be a cup of tea in the dressing-room after the game.

DON: Is that all?

JERRY: Then he said his team was the best in the school and my team couldn't lick the mixed infants.

DON: The mixed infants, hey?

JERRY: Yes, the nerve of it! So then I just tried to brush a fly off his nose, and he hit me right in the eye.

DON: And that, I suppose, ended your conversation?

JERRY: Not exactly, because then I fell over and accidentally kicked him on the shin. So he twisted my arm right round the back of my neck.

DON: That was a bit off, wasn't it?

JERRY: Then as he left me lying on the ground, he said he

wasn't going to be my friend anymore, and I said, 'And I shan't speak to you again,' and that's it.

DON: That means you won't let him play with your race-track anymore.

JERRY: I certainly shan't.

DON: And I suppose you won't be allowed to borrow his fishing-rod and catch your uncle's gold-fish again.

JERRY: I suppose not.

DON: But if you're in the same class as Sidney at school, you can't really stop speaking to him, can you?

JERRY: I shall just have to go on calling him a wally and things like that.

DON: Well, that isn't going to help, is it? Think of the chaos in our homes and schools, let alone the world, if we all went round insulting each other like that.

JERRY: Well, I think Sidney's no good and I don't like him.

DON: You know, Jerry, if you don't tame a tiger cub when it is young and harmless it will grow up into a ferocious and dangerous animal. And if you don't learn to forgive, and conquer your dislikes now while you're young, they'll develop into hatred and bitterness as the years go by. And nobody wants to be friends with a person who hates.

JERRY: I don't think I should like that.

DON: Well, don't you think the best thing would be for you to make it up with Sidney and be friends again?

JERRY: We did use to have a lot of fun together. Like that time we hid a hedgehog in his sister's handbag. She said if he did it again she would stick it down his neck, and I shouldn't like to miss that.

DON: I'm sure you wouldn't. Do you know, Jerry, it's just like that with God.

JERRY: He hasn't got a sister, has he?

DON: No, of course not, but he has got a lot of friends, and many have quarrelled with him. They are not on speaking terms and will have nothing to do with him.

JERRY: Surely it's not God's fault, is it? I mean, he doesn't hate anyone, does he?

DON: Certainly not. In fact he sent the Lord Jesus to show us how much he cares about us. What's more, he can take away the bad things which spoil our lives, so we can be friends with God again, instead of being against him.

JERRY: I should think he's the best sort of friend to have.

DON: He certainly is. The Bible tells us he sticks even closer in his friendships than the closest of relations.

JERRY: You can't get closer than that. I think perhaps I'd better go round and see Sidney after all. Cheerio.

DON: Cheerio, Jerry.

Between you, me and the gatepost, man was made for friendships and he can't live a full life without them, so they are worth hanging on to. Man was made for God as well, and he can't live a full life without him either. Goodbye.

# PART THREE

## *Sketches for Family Services and School Assemblies*

# *A The Christian Year*

## 11 The King is Coming

THEME

The danger of being so busy preparing for Christmas that we forget what we are preparing for. (Luke 3:4–6.)

CAST

Two friends—DAVE and KATHY—who are excitable types feeding off each other's ideas and enthusiasm.

COSTUME AND PROPS

Several long strands of tinsel or streamers.
A bowl of nuts and a bowl of crisps.
Six balloons.
Party music.
DAVE and KATHY wear jeans and T-shirts.

SCRIPT

*Enter* DAVE *and* KATHY *from opposite sides*

KATHY: Dave, Dave! [*Gasping for air*]
DAVE: What is it Kathy?
KATHY: The King is coming...he's coming to town!
DAVE: No?
KATHY: Yes.
DAVE: What here?
KATHY: Yes, I've just heard.
DAVE: When's he coming?
KATHY: On the 25th.
DAVE: That's great. We'll have to hold a celebration.
KATHY: A huge banquet.
DAVE: A disco.

KATHY: With loads of flashing lights.
DAVE: A party.
KATHY: Games, balloons....
DAVE: There's so much to prepare. Decorate!
KATHY: Yes, this place could do with a new coat of paint.
DAVE: No, not that type of decorate. I mean streamers, golden hanging stars, glittering globes, bells and tinsel.
KATHY: Right, let's start preparing! You organise the games and the food, and I'll get working on the decorations and disco.
DAVE: Right, I need six volunteers to help me decorate.

*DAVE will have to ad-lib organising the volunteers who have to hold up the tinsel or streamers between them. This can be at the front standing on chairs arranged for them or even on their own chairs, as long as they can stay that way for the rest of the sketch.*

DAVE: That looks great! This is going to be terrific with all these decorations. I feel in a party mood already!

*Enter KATHY with two bowls of crisps and nuts.*

KATHY: Hey! This looks brilliant! I've got some nuts and crisps which we can pass round. Have one.
DAVE: Thanks. Not bad.
KATHY: Would you like one? [*KATHY then starts to hand them out round the congregation.*]
DAVE: Don't give out too many or we won't have any left for the celebration.
KATHY: I think we've already started. But what about the disco?
DAVE: Oh yes, I'll need some more people to be flashing lights.
KATHY: I'll get some music on. [*Exit to play a short burst of music.*]

*DAVE then gets at least four volunteers to stand up on stage facing the congregation in pairs holding their hands up to be the flashing lights. A quick demonstration of opening and closing hands might help to show the flashing. Extra movements to the music should prove amusing as well.*

KATHY: [*Enters when the music stops.*] That's good, but we need some party games to make the celebrations go with a real swing.

DAVE: What have you in mind?

KATHY: A balloon game! [*Pulls out six balloons.*] Now all we need is six people with a lot of puff to blow these balloons up. [*Hands them out to volunteers.*]

DAVE: We've got the balloons but we don't know what the game is.

KATHY: It's quite simple. This half [*gestures to one half of the congregation*] is against this half [*indicates the other half.*] And neither side must let the balloons touch the ground.

DAVE: Let's have a trial run! I'll put some more music on. [*Exit to play rest of music.*]

KATHY: Balloons at the ready? Music at the ready?

DAVE: Ready!

KATHY: On your marks...GO!

*Music starts and at the end of the track the game stops with the balloons being collected in. Enter DAVE.*

DAVE: That was great fun. This is going to be the best celebration ever! Celebrating...Celebrating? What are we going to celebrate again?

KATHY: You know.

DAVE: No.

KATHY: Well it's er...do you know in all this excitement I've forgotten.

DAVE: But you were the one who came rushing in getting us all preparing the celebrations.

KATHY: I know that, we're preparing for...? Can't you remember anything I said?

DAVE: Sure, there was a date.

KATHY: What date?

DAVE: The 1st?

KATHY: No.

DAVE: The 14th?

KATHY: No, no.

DAVE: The 31st!

KATHY: No, it was something in the twenties.

DAVE: I remember—it was the 25th.

KATHY: That was it, the 25th.
[*Slowly.*] And...on...the...25th—the King is coming to town!

DAVE: The King's coming! That was it, yes!

KATHY: Now fancy that! What a thing to forget!

DAVE: It was all these exciting preparations.

KATHY: [*Turning towards congregation.*] In this exciting time of Advent, you won't forget who you're preparing for, will you?

*Colin Mengell*

# 12 The Trip of a Lifetime

THEME

The Bible is the official guide to the kingdom of heaven. (2 Timothy 3:15–17.)

CAST

Travel Agent, polite and precise.
Young Man, angry.

COSTUME

Traditional as far as practical.

PROPS

The Travel Agent should be sitting at a desk with a telephone, some travel brochures, a Bible and, if possible, a computer.

SCRIPT

TRAVEL AGENT: [*Dials number on telephone.*] Hello, is that Mrs Jones? Hello, this is the Good News Travel Agency here. Hello, yes, just to let you know, your reservations have been confirmed. Isn't it wonderful? Yes, I know. You feel like you've started a new life, don't you? Yes I know, everyone says that. Yes. All right, then. 'Bye. [*Puts down phone.*]

YOUNG MAN: [*Entering.*] Hey! Hello there. You a travel agent?

TRAVEL AGENT: Yes, that's right. Hello. How can I help you?

YOUNG MAN: Look, I want to go somewhere. Do you know what I mean?

TRAVEL AGENT: Yes, of course. Where would you like to go?

YOUNG MAN: Well, somewhere different, you know. I've

travelled everywhere, but, well, I want to go somewhere different—you know—make sense of my life.

TRAVEL AGENT: Oh, I see.

YOUNG MAN: I've tried everything, but I still feel like, well, you know, sort of chewed up inside. I really need to sort things out—thought I might go off somewhere.

TRAVEL AGENT: [*Opening brochures.*] I see, well, um, let's just think. What about the South of France? Have you been to the South of France?

YOUNG MAN: Yeah, of course I've been there. Monte Carlo. Crazy place. Went with a new girl every night—you know. But, well, after a while, they're all the same. Doesn't mean a thing anymore.

TRAVEL AGENT: I see. Well, what about California? Hollywood. You could go to Hollywood.

YOUNG MAN: No, I've done that. Couldn't take it, really. Hollywood. Those guys are so rich. Just eats me up. And the tour guide was a creep, huh!

TRAVEL AGENT: Yes, I see. Well, what about somewhere more exotic? Ah, yes, here we are. Yes—Katmandu. Have you ever thought about Katmandu?

YOUNG MAN: Katmandu. No, not again. That's where I got into drugs. Hash, Speed, you know, the lot. Some trips, eh. Every day. But it's no fun. [*Pensive.*] Not now. No, no. I'd stop if I could. No more trips. Be great.

TRAVEL AGENT: I see. Well, is there anywhere else here you'd like to look at?

YOUNG MAN: Look, I've done all that stuff. But listen, what's the point of life? Eh? The kicks aren't kicks anymore. Where can I go?

TRAVEL AGENT: [*Picking up Bible.*] Listen. There *is* a very special destination. Something you might be interested in. It's called the kingdom of heaven.

YOUNG MAN: Heaven? Hey, where are you coming from? I'm not ready to die yet.

TRAVEL AGENT: Oh, you don't have to die to go to the kingdom of heaven.

YOUNG MAN: What do you mean? I'll go to heaven when I die.

TRAVEL AGENT: Not unless you go to the kingdom of heaven here first, while you're still alive.

YOUNG MAN: Oh? Well how do I get there then? It's not in all the stuff.

TRAVEL AGENT: [*Handing over Bible.*] No, all the details are in this special catalogue.

YOUNG MAN: Let's have a look then. Do they have any good swimming pools? Hey, there are no pictures.

TRAVEL AGENT: No. No swimming pools. No hotels. No beaches.

YOUNG MAN: That's not very good. How much does it cost?

TRAVEL AGENT: It's free.

YOUNG MAN: Free? That's better! What do you get?

TRAVEL AGENT: You get a life that's full of love, and of joy, and of peace. That's what you really need in life, you know.

YOUNG MAN: Cor, yeah, I can see that. Yeah, that's what I need. When can I go?

TRAVEL AGENT: You can go whenever you want. But there are certain travel restrictions.

YOUNG MAN: Oh?

TRAVEL AGENT: Yes, you can't take anything with you.

YOUNG MAN: Oh, I travel light anyway. I just take—well you know—what I need—you know—to, er, get on.

TRAVEL AGENT: No, you must leave everything behind. Lust, envy, guilt, greed, drugs—everything.

YOUNG MAN: Hey, I can't do that, really. I've tried giving it all up, but I can't.

TRAVEL AGENT: No, you probably can't. But you'll have a good tour guide—to help you.

YOUNG MAN: Yeah, who's that, then?

TRAVEL AGENT: His name is Jesus.

YOUNG MAN: Jesus? Hey, he was quite a guy, wasn't he? But how can *he* help *me*?

TRAVEL AGENT: It's simple. Have you ever done anything that's wrong?

YOUNG MAN: Yeah, I guess so. Lots o' things.

TRAVEL AGENT: Well you must just get down on your knees, and talk to Jesus just like we're talking now, and just honestly say, 'I'm sorry, please forgive me,' and then ask him to be your guide.

YOUNG MAN: Hey, well, that sounds OK. Is that it? You sure?

TRAVEL AGENT: That's it. Promise. Here's the catalogue.

YOUNG MAN: [*Starting to leave.*] Fantastic! Great! Well, thanks then. See you again.

TRAVEL AGENT: Let me know how you get on. Have a nice trip.

*Peter Heywood*

# 13 Who is Christmas For?

## THEME

The Christmas message is for everyone. This is a short drama for use in family worship. Staging and learning of words is kept to the minimum. The use of rhyme is a deliberate aid to learning and is especially helpful when working with young children or when production time is short. However, care is needed in practising voice inflections and in ensuring understanding of the character played so that the necessary expression may be given to the words and the dah-de-dah repetition so often found when speaking in rhyme may be avoided.

## CAST AND COSTUMES

NUMBER—As many children as would like to take part plus one adult, teenager or older child with a good speaking voice as the Narrator.
NARRATOR—Needs to be well chosen and to have the children's confidence.
CHORUS—As many children as you wish in ordinary clothes.
ADULT VOICE—Speaks from the congregation.
SHEPHERDS AND WISE MEN
MARY and JOSEPH—In traditional dress. Quite young children may take these parts.
MUM—Scarf on head and rollers in hair, pinafore, mixing bowl and spoon.
DAD—Long trousers, moustache, pullover, slippers, carrying newspaper, pipe in mouth.
TEENAGER—Any way-out teenage dress, eg, lots of big earrings, leathers, coloured hair, etc.
GRANDMA—Old-fashioned granny outfit, walking-stick or frame, carrying knitting.
FOREIGN CHILD—Choose your own country, eg, Pakistan, India, Africa, Jamaica.
HOMELESS PERSON—Dirty, old torn clothes, paper or plastic carrier bag.
CHILDREN—As many as you wish, dressed for bed and carrying stuffed Christmas stockings.

## STAGE SETTING

Improvisation is necessary here as much will depend on the church building in which the drama is to take place. A crib scene, ie, a manger with baby and a seat for Mary should be prominent in the background. One stage block and steps of the type found in many primary schools and sited on the chancel steps would be suitable for this. Other seats, steps and blocks to be grouped around and in front of the crib scene for other characters to take their places as they appear, and to sit, stand or kneel as appropriate. The choir-stalls themselves and the pulpit steps and lectern may also be used for positioning characters as the final tableau is built up. The centre aisle should be kept clear for access, likewise if the church has no centre aisle the two side aisles could be used instead. Narrator enters the pulpit while a medley of Christmas music is played. The small chorus may be grouped at the foot of the pulpit or on the front row of the congregation. Other characters out of sight to enter from right or left as the producer wishes. Children with stockings come quietly into church once the congregation has settled and the service started, to sit unobtrusively at the back of the congregation, or they may remain in the porch or out of sight until needed.

## SCRIPT

*Music—a Christmas medley.*

| | |
|---|---|
| NARRATOR: | [*Enters pulpit.*] Who is Christmas for? |
| CHORUS: | Who is Christmas for? |
| | [*Enter Mary and Joseph from right.*] |
| JOSEPH: | Christmas was for Mary, Joseph and the babe, |
| | The shepherds and wise men with presents lade, |
| | [*Enter shepherds and three wise men. They bow to the baby and take up positions in the crib scene.*] |
| | The angels and people of Bethlehem. |
| | [*Mary and Joseph take up positions at the manger.*] |
| NARRATOR: | Yes, the people living then |
| | They believed the things they saw |
| | But now who is Christmas for? |
| CHORUS: | Who is Christmas for? |

ADULT VOICE: Christmas is for the children.

[*Children enter from West end in night clothes, carrying Christmas stockings. Skip down centre aisle while singing Jingle Bells or other Christmas song.*]

1ST CHILD: We love the feel of stockings big,
Of lights on tree and Christmas crib.

2ND CHILD: We love the baby Jesus small
For he was born to save us all.

3RD CHILD: His is the birthday we celebrate,
Hurry to the manger—we mustn't be late.
[*Children take up positions round the crib scene or in the choir stalls.*]

NARRATOR: Yes, the children believe.
The Christmas joy
Touches the heart of each girl and boy.
Yet who else, who else is Christmas for?

CHORUS: (including the other children now) Who else is Christmas for?
[*Enter Mum from side carrying mixing bowl and spoon, looking suitably harrassed.*]

MUM: Not for me, not for me.
Turkey for dinner and trifle for tea,
Presents to buy and parcels to send,
Cards to write, jobs without end.
Keeping the peace when they squabble and fight;
Are Auntie and Uncle and Granny all right?
No, for me it's not much fun.
A woman's work is never done.

NARRATOR: But yes, it is for you.
You can find the wonder too.
Go to the manger and stable bare.
Take all your worries and leave them there.
For *his* is the birthday we celebrate.

MUM: I'll hurry to the manger—I mustn't be late.
[*Mum takes up position in crib scene.*]

NARRATOR: The Son of God, born for all men
Who else is Christmas for then?

CHORUS: Who else, who else is Christmas for?
[*Enter Dad from side with newspaper, slippers and pipe, looking fed up.*]

DAD: Not for me, not for me.
Too many visitors and folk for a drink.
It costs too much—that's what I think.
Head that aches and stomach sore,
My pocket feeling very poor.
Hearing old jokes no longer funny.
It's just an excuse for making money.

NARRATOR: Oh yes, it is for you
You can find the wonder too.
Go to the manger and stable bare.
Take your lost dreams and leave them there.
For *his* is the birthday we celebrate.

DAD: I'll hurry to the manger,
I mustn't be late.
[*Dad moves to take up position in crib scene.*]

NARRATOR: Lying in the stable, the infant sweet.
Who else, who else is the baby to meet?

CHORUS: Who else is Christmas for?
[*Enter teenager from side, carrying records or guitar.*]

TEENAGER: Not for me, not for me.
I go my own way.
Don't listen now to what older folk say.
I don't even know if it's all true,
Grown-ups don't show it in what they do.
[*Pause.*]
Yet I wonder, and try to think things out.
I wonder what living is all about.

NARRATOR: Go to the manger, kneel in prayer.
You too will find your answer there.
Take your questions to the infant sweet.
Lay them down at the baby's feet.
For *his* is the birthday we celebrate.

TEENAGER: I'll hurry to the manger,
I mustn't be late.
[*Teenager moves to take up position in crib scene.*]

NARRATOR: To the Christ child the King
Who else shall we bring.
Who else, who else is Christmas for?

CHORUS: Who else is Christmas for?
[*Enter Granny with her knitting and walking-stick or frame.*]

GRANNY: Not for me, not for me.
I used to enjoy the Christmas fun.
Now those days are over and done.
The good times, they've long since gone
Since my daughter grew up and so did my son.
Now I'm alone, only the past to share
[*Pause.*]
Who cares for me? For whom can I care?

NARRATOR: This Christmas is for you.
The love of God stays all life through.
Go take your memories to the stable bare.
Take them to the manger and leave them there.
For *his* is the birthday we celebrate.

GRANNY: I'll hurry to the manger,
I mustn't be late.
[*Granny moves to position in crib scene.*]

NARRATOR: The young folk and the old
For who else is the story told?
Who else is Christmas for?

CHORUS: Who else is Christmas for?
[*Enter foreign child.*]

FOREIGN CHILD: Not for me, not for me.
I don't belong here you see.
I'm different from other girls and boys.
Brought from a land that's far away,
A land where it's hot nearly every day.
You don't understand all I do or say.
I'm a stranger here in every way.

NARRATOR: Christmas is for you.
Black and white and yellow too.
It matters not the colour of skin.
Go to the baby and kneel to him.
For *his* is the birthday we celebrate.

FOREIGN CHILD: I'll hurry to the manger.
I mustn't be late.
[*Moves to position in the crib scene.*]

NARRATOR: An immigrant child from distant land.
To whom else does the babe hold out his hand?
Who else is Christmas for?

CHORUS: Who else is Christmas for?

HOMELESS PERSON: Not for me, not for me.
I've nowhere to sleep,
Nowhere to go.
I see a room lit with Christmas glow,
But no one cares or wants to know.
No family with me is happy to share,
Mine's a park bench or a basement stair.
No room for me anywhere.

NARRATOR: There is room for you
Near One who knows
What it feels like left out in the cold.
No welcome for him on earth—
Just a stable to greet his birth.
The only place to lay his head
A trough in the wall where the animals fed.
Folk celebrate his birthday without him there.
They have no time with him to share.
So go to the manger.

HOMELESS PERSON: I mustn't be late
For his is the birthday we celebrate.
[*Homeless person takes up position in the crib scene.*]

NARRATOR: Look at the crib,

CHORUS: Look at the crib.

NARRATOR: See the people there.
Mary, Joseph, shepherds too—
Ordinary folk, like me and you.
Wise men, with gifts costly and rare.
All kneeling in the stable bare.
Just like that Christmas the first of all
When poor men heard the angels call.

ALL: So hurry to the manger.
*You* mustn't be late [*pointing at the congregation*]
For his is the birthday we celebrate.

[*The children move quietly down the centre aisle to the back of the church during the singing of a suitable advent or Christmas hymn or while appropriate music is played. Seats should be reserved for them at the back so that they can share in the rest of the service.*] Suitable hymns—'Hark the glad sound the Saviour comes'; 'Thou didst leave thy throne'.

*Margaret Marr*

# 14 The Reluctant Shepherd

THEME

The Christmas story from the possible point of view of one of the shepherds, to encourage faith. (Luke 2:8–20.)

CAST

Two shepherds, 1 and 2.

COSTUME

Traditional clothes or T-shirt and jeans.

SCRIPT

[*Sounds of sheep bleating.*]

1: I never wanted to be a shepherd.
2: No?
1: No, I wanted to be a real estate investment analyst.
2: Didn't get enough exams, eh?
1: No, just couldn't spell 'analyst'. Well, I could spell it, just couldn't spell it correctly that's all. I mean, what's a silent 'Q' between friends? I mean who would work with sheep out of choice?
2: I would, but then I had to.
1: Oh well, that's different. Mindless creatures, sheep. Look at them all, following each other round everywhere.
2: Like sheep, really.
1: They are sheep.
2: Well, that would account for it, wouldn't it?
1: Still it could be worse. Not many jobs pay you to lie on your back and stare at the stars all night.
2: No, not many jobs pay you this badly, though.
1: True. Looking at those stars reminds me of that night.
2: What night?
1: That night. That was a night that was.
2: Was it.

1: Aye. That was a real night, all dark it were... and...

2: Often happens with nights, they say.

1: Yeah, but this weren't no ordinary night.

2: No?

1: No, a night and a half it were, well it were the same length as most nights for the time of year, but you know what I mean?

2: No, I don't think I do.

1: You remember, the night we saw the... the thingy?

2: Oh, here we go again. We've been through this before, I wasn't here, remember?

1: Oh yeah. You were down the laundrette washing the socks by night.

2: Yeah well, it's cheaper rates on the night shift, isn't it?

1: Anyway. We was all sitting down minding our own business.

2: The sheep.

1: Yeah, minding the sheep, when somebody turned the sun back on. Well, that's what it seemed like. It was so bright I thought someone had done a sneaky and invented electricity. Once we'd come out from hiding behind the sheep, and our eyes adjusted like, we saw this huge angel glowing like a great big Ready Brek advert, only different. Come to think about it, very different—in fact it were so different there were nothing like it, but I tell you it were frightening. He told us not to panic. I thought, it's all right him saying that, he must meet angels every day of his life. Then he told us that there were a baby being born down in the town.

2: Oh big deal. That's a bit over the top isn't it? Haven't they got anything better to do with their time? There's babies born down there every night.

1: Yeah, but this weren't no ordinary baby. We'd find this one lying in a feeding trough.

2: Well, admittedly that's a bit different.

1: No, that didn't come out right. This baby was the one we've been waiting for, the one to set us all free—the Messiah.

2: So why did they tell a bunch of shepherds?

1: I don't know. Ask them.

2: I can't, they've gone.

1: Anyway, just as the novelty of seeing an angel was wearing off, he was joined by a huge choir of his mates, thousands of them all flying around, singing their hearts out to God. It was incredible, better than any Eisteddfod I've been to.

2: So what did you do?

1: Well we left the sheep, and went to see the baby, like we was told.

2: So that's why when I came back with the socks, the sheep were running round like sheep without a shepherd, if you see what I mean.

1: Yeah, we were down seeing the Saviour.

2: And you expect me to believe that? Look, if you want to slope off duty that's fine, but don't try and make up these stories to get yourself off the hook afterwards.

1: But it's true.

2: I think you've flipped your lid. To think that I'd believe a story like that. You must be crazy, off your trolley, lost your marbles.

1: No I'm not, at least, they were all there last time I counted them.

2: I think you've been spending too long with these sheep. You've gone mad—'allucinationing, happeritions, talking to the sheep. Next thing you'll know you'll be sounding like them.

1: Baaa.

*Trapdoor Theatre Company*

# 15 Christmas Card

## THEME

To stress that the Christmas story is not a fairy story. It is intended for children four to nine and would be suitable for either school (hence reference to headteacher) or church. More pantomime elements according to taste.

## CAST AND COSTUMES

SHOPPER in modern dress, MARY and JOSEPH in traditional costume. Mary should carry a baby which should probably be a doll.

## PROPS

A simple frame needs to be constructed so that when Mary and Joseph enter they appear to become part of a Christmas card. The remaining props are indicated in the script.

## SCRIPT

Children sing a well-known carol while MARY, JOSEPH and baby enter and take up their position in the frame.

SHOPPER: [*Singing the carol for a bar or two.*] Hello. I've been Christmas shopping, and I've bought lots of lovely lovely food, and lots and lots of lovely lovely drink, and lots and lots and lots of lovely lovely lovely presents. Have you bought me a present? Haven't you? Why not? [*Plenty of opportunity to ad-lib.*] Well shall I show you the presents I've bought? Shall I? I bought a lovely chicken. [*brings out rubber chicken, possibly with green slime in mouth.*] Oh dear, doesn't seem very well, does it? Well, I got a nice present for your Headteacher. It's a book called *How to make Rat Stew*. But she already had a copy, so I bought her these instead [*brings out long johns*]. Then a flower that squirts, [*more silly presents according to taste*]. Now then, the only thing I haven't got is Christmas cards. Can you see them on sale anywhere?

[*The children, with any luck, point to the tableau that the Holy Family have formed. A sign saying 'Buy your Christmas cards here' might help.*]

Oh yes, so they are. Well, isn't that nice? That's what I call a lovely card. A nice traditional card with Mary, Joseph and the baby. What a pretty picture. Makes me feel all nice and warm and cosy inside. I don't think I need to look any further. I'll buy fifty of these.

[*While he's facing the front, JOSEPH takes a hammer-shaped implement out of his cloak and hits SHOPPER over the head. MARY lifts up a card with 'Zap' on it.*]

SHOPPER: What the...was that you? Well it must have been one of you on the front row. Did you see who it was? Who was it then? Joseph? Which form is he in? *That* Joseph? Now come on, I may look old but I wasn't born yesterday. Pull the other one. That Joseph isn't real. He's just a person on a Christmas card. He's just part of a story. Are you trying to tell me that he came out of the Christmas card and banged me over the head? I've never heard such nonsense in all my life. If that's the sort of school this is I'm not going to waste my time here. I'm off.

[*As he moves off, MARY takes JOSEPH's crook and trips up the SHOPPER, who somersaults and lands in a custard pie which MARY has thrown in front of him. JOSEPH raises board marked 'Ouch!'*]

SHOPPER: Come on. Who was it? Headteacher, I'm going to have to report this school. It's absolutely disgraceful. Who was it who tripped me up? Mary? Is she a teacher? *That* Mary? Look, she's not real. She's just part of a story. She can't just come out of a Christmas card. Are you trying to tell me that Joseph and Mary are real? Oh no, they're not [*etc.*]. All right, I'll find out for myself. [*Goes up to prod JOSEPH.*] See, he didn't move. [*Goes over to MARY, and as he does so JOSEPH tickles his ear with a feather.*]

SHOPPER: Have you got fleas in this school? [*Turns away again, and again JOSEPH tickles him.*] Who did that? He didn't! Well, why can't you do it when I'm looking at you. Go on. Show me you're real. [*MARY yawns.*]

SHOPPER: I don't believe it. I must be seeing things. You're not really real. [*Leans forward. MARY says 'Boo,' and fires water pistol at him. Exit SHOPPER.*]

MARY: Joseph.

JOSEPH: Mmm?

MARY: I get fed up with people saying we're not real.

JOSEPH: So do I.

MARY: I mean; I get fed up with being on Christmas cards so people think we're part of some fairy story.

JOSEPH: So do I.

MARY: I get right fed up.

JOSEPH: So do I.

MARY: Go and change the baby and then we'll take him out for some fresh air. What's the matter? [*To audience.*] Don't tell me *you* don't think we're real, either.

*Jabbok Theatre*

# 16 Star

## THEME

Christmas or Epiphany based on Matthew 2:1–12.

## CAST

Three actors or actresses to play 'stars' (as in *The Sky at Night*).

The Stars can be played by children or adults, male or female. The GLUM STAR sounds a bit like the late Les Dawson (older, disappointed and gloomy) while the NEW STAR sounds like a little girl at a birthday party, very pleased with herself. The GROOVY STAR could sound a bit like an enthusiastic disc jockey or a trying-to-be-trendy teenager.

## COSTUME AND PROPS

Each star can carry a little stick on the end of which is a tinsel star. They could wear more elaborate costumes.

## SCRIPT

*Note:* When this was written, 'wicked' was the current slang for anything really trendy, exciting, cool and marvellous. If the word is no longer current, or not in use in your locality, I'd urge you to try and adapt the sketch with an up-to-date or different expression. This may mean you have to play around with the tag-line slightly, but it would be worth the effort as this sketch does play extremely well, and is also easy to perform.

There is an optional scene-setting prologue, which can be spoken by the leader of the service, but the sketch is equally effective without it.

*Optional prologue*

When the baby Jesus was born, we are told that a new star appeared in the sky. Have you ever wondered how the *other* stars felt about this?

[*Two stars enter, chatting idly.*]

GROOVY STAR: It's great, isn't it?
GLUM STAR: What is?
GROOVY STAR: Being a star. Up here in the sky. Twinkling.
GLUM STAR: It's all right, I suppose.
GROOVY STAR: I mean, look at the wonderful view!
GLUM STAR: The wonderful view? What's so wonderful about it? It's just the same as it's always been? Other stars like us. Distant galaxies. A few asteroids. The odd planet. The occasional moon. It never changes.
GROOVY STAR: What about Halley's Comet, then, eh?
GLUM STAR: Halley's Comet? Well, that only comes round about once every seventy-four years. It's hardly a regular fixture, is it?
GROOVY STAR: That's wicked, is Halley's Comet. Wick*ed*.
GLUM STAR: And it never stops to have a little chat, does it? Just rushes around the universe, scattering astral dust everywhere. Oh, well, that's comets for you.

[*New star slowly enters.*]

GLUM STAR: One day it'll just burn itself out, you mark my words.
GROOVY STAR: Hey, what's that?
GLUM STAR: What's what?
GROOVY STAR: [*Pointing.*] Look—over there—it's something new.
GLUM STAR: Something new? What do you mean, something new?
NEW STAR: [*Waving.*] Hello.
GROOVY STAR: [*Waving back enthusiastically.*] Hello!
NEW STAR: I'm a new star.
GLUM STAR: A new star? How can you be a new star?
NEW STAR: I don't know, I just am. [*Proudly.*] I was made by God.
GLUM STAR: [*Defensively.*] Yes, well so were *we*, you know. We were all made by God.
NEW STAR: Oh, were you? Well, I was made for a special purpose.
GROOVY STAR: Hey, that's really wicked! What is it—what's your special purpose?

NEW STAR: To guide people.

GLUM STAR: Guide people? We've been guiding people for years! Guiding travellers across the desert, guiding sailors over the sea. That's what stars *do*—guide people.

NEW STAR: But I've got to guide some special people.

GLUM STAR: Everything's special with you, isn't it? Well, perhaps, special new star, you will kindly tell us ordinary old stars who these special people are you've got to guide.

NEW STAR: I've got to guide three wise men to find a baby.

GROOVY STAR: A baby! Hey, that's really wicked!

GLUM STAR: Three wise men? They can't be very wise if they need a star to help them find a baby.

NEW STAR: But it's a special baby.

GLUM STAR: Oh, I might have known. All right, then, what's so special about this baby?

NEW STAR: It's a royal baby.

GROOVY STAR: A royal baby? Hey, that's *royal* wicked!

NEW STAR: It's a baby king. And he's not just the king of one country. He's the king of all the worlds and all the planets and all the moons and all the universe and everything!

GLUM STAR: Yes, well I suppose that is fairly special.

GROOVY STAR: Wow! The king of everything?

NEW STAR: Everything.

GROOVY STAR: Even Halley's Comet?

NEW STAR: Even Halley's Comet.

GROOVY STAR: Hey, that's wick*ed*!

NEW STAR: No—it's God!

[*Blackout, if possible. Otherwise they pause for a moment, all raise their sticks together, then take a bow.*]

*Philip Glassborow*

# 17 Happy Families

THEME

To illustrate the problems of the wrong priorities in family life.

CAST

MUM, DAD and BOY, all conventionally dressed: MUM in apron, DAD with books and pen, BOY with toy needing repair.

SCRIPT

MUM: Darling, how long are you going to be?
DAD: I told you, just another five minutes.
MUM: That was a quarter of an hour ago.
DAD: How can I concentrate when you keep giving me a running commentary on how that blasted meal's doing?
MUM: Well it's burnt now!
DAD: Some things are more important than a stupid chicken.
MUM: That 'stupid chicken chasseur' has taken me two-and-a-half hours to make.
DAD: Just give me two minutes.
BOY: Dad.
MUM: Jonathan, don't disturb your father. He's busy.
BOY: But I want him to mend my—
MUM: [*Interrupting.*] We're just about to have din-dins.
BOY: But if it's broken I won't be able to—
MUM: I'll try and get Daddy to look at it after [*changing tone to get at father*], if he can find the time.
BOY: But I want him to do it now.
MUM: Not now. Daddy hasn't got time for anything. Maybe I'll have a look at it later.
DAD: Cracked it. That's a good job done. I told you it wouldn't take long. You've got to hand it to me, I've just got it.
MUM: Got what? No time for your family?
DAD: That's not fair.
BOY: Dad.
DAD: It's important to get these figures balanced, especially if I'm ever going to get Malcolm's job.

MUM: You have to have success at any price, don't you?
BOY: Mum.
MUM: We all know what your priority is.
DAD: So what's the fuss then?
BOY: Dad, I want you to—
DAD: Not now, Jonathan.
MUM: Why can't you leave it at work? I hate you cooking the books at home here. You're burning the candle at both ends.
DAD: I may cook the books, but you're the authority on burning.
MUM: Maybe, but what if you burn out?
BOY: Mum, I want you to—
MUM: I told you, I'll look at it later.
DAD: You're just jealous 'cos I'm successful at what I do.
BOY: Dad, I want you to—
DAD: Jonathan!
MUM: I'm not jealous. Some of us would prefer to fail.
DAD: I bet!
MUM: I would. If that's the price of success.
DAD: And what's *that* supposed to mean?
MUM: Because of your precious work you haven't spent one hour with the children all week. They've almost forgotten who you are.
DAD: But they know who pays for their food and clothes. And who took them to the Algarve last year?
MUM: And some family holiday that turned out to be.
DAD: Well, I didn't know the boss was going to be there.
MUM: No, not until the week before.
BOY: Dad.
DAD: Well I have to make a good impression.
BOY: Dad, I want—
DAD: I can't afford to lose my job.
BOY: Dad, I want you to—
DAD: I've got a wife and family to support.
MUM: Not for long.
BOY: Dad.
DAD: What *is* it, Jonathan?
BOY: Dad, I want you and Mummy to stop arguing.

*Trapdoor Theatre Company*

# 18 The Passion

## THEME

A biblical mosaic leading up to the crucifixion, using a mixture of mime and dialogue.

## CAST

NARRATOR, JESUS, PETER, and seven in CHORUS who play various parts.

## COSTUME

Traditional, but with discretion in the case of Adam and Eve (!) or all T-shirts and jeans.

## PROPS

Centre-back, a stepladder with Jesus standing at top. Fruit (not necessarily an apple) on a rung halfway up. Curled up on floor in front of steps, two of the chorus as Adam and Eve.

## SCRIPT

NARRATOR: In the beginning, God created the heavens
And the earth.
in the beginning, God created man in his likeness.
In the image of God he created them.
Male and female he created them.
[*ADAM and EVE slowly stand.*]
Forming them from the dust of the ground
[*Fully standing, heads down.*]
And breathing into their nostrils the breath of life.
[*ADAM and EVE raise their heads to look at each other.*]
And man became a living being.
[*They raise downstage hands and lightly touch palms.*]
Made perfect to enjoy God for ever.
[*Explore. EVE finds fruit. Bites into it.*]
But man rebelled against God.

[*She offers the fruit to ADAM.*]
Breaking his one command.
[*ADAM bites into fruit.*]
Rejecting his free offer of love.
[*Fruit thrown away in disgust. ADAM and EVE move stage right, facing centre. CHORUS enters to slow drum beat. Expressionless. Take up positions covering stage. Face ADAM and EVE.*]
And when Adam sinned, sin entered the entire human race.
When Adam sinned, his sin spread death throughout all the world.
When Adam sinned, everything began to grow old and die.

CHORUS: For we have all sinned.
We have all gone astray.
We have all rejected God.

NARRATOR: And are cut off from him.
[*Turn backs to JESUS.*]
And from each other.
[*Turn to first position: head down, cross hands at wrist. In the following sequence, ADAM and EVE move through the CHORUS. At each concept, they touch a member of the CHORUS who collapses.*]
Nations at war.
Catholics and Protestants.
Families divided.
Black and white.
Rich world, poor world.
And without the shedding of blood there is no forgiveness.
But God so loved the world that he gave.
He gave his only son, Jesus.
[*JESUS descends the ladder and moves to centre stage.*]
Who made himself nothing,
Taking the form of a servant,
Being made in human likeness.
[*As each category is listed, the corpses of the CHORUS revive and take up an attitude of worship.*]

JESUS: The spirit of the Lord is upon me
Because he has anointed me to bring good news

to the suffering,
Good news to the afflicted.
He has sent me to comfort the broken-hearted,
To announce liberty to captives,
To open the eyes of the blind,
And to preach good news to the poor.

NARRATOR: But we despised him and rejected him.
[*Tableau: arrest of JESUS and PETER's denial.*]
And Peter said

PETER: I don't know what you're talking about.

NARRATOR: A man of sorrows, acquainted with bitterest grief.
He swore to them

PETER: I tell you I don't know him.

CHORUS: Yet it was our grief he bore,
Our sorrows that weighed him down.
And he was wounded
And bruised
For our
Sins.
He was lashed.
And we are healed.

NARRATOR: They wove a crown of thorns, and thrust it on his head, mocking him:

CHORUS: Hail, King of the Jews!

NARRATOR: He was brought as a lamb to the slaughter
And as a sheep before her shearers is dumb
So he stood silent before the ones condemning him.
[*Tableau: Pilate washes his hands.*]
From prison and trial, they led him away to his death.
They came to Golgotha. There, they crucified him.
[*JESUS is lashed to a crosspiece. Loud hammer blows.*]

JESUS: Father! Forgive them!
[*He is hauled up steps and hung from rung near top.*]

NARRATOR: Those who passed by hurled insults at him, shaking their heads.

CHORUS: He saved others, but can't save himself!
Come on then! Come down from the cross and we'll believe you.
He said, 'I am the Son of God.'

Well then, let God rescue him now—
If he wants him.

NARRATOR: But who among the people of that day realised it was their sins he was dying for: that he was suffering their punishment?

JESUS: My God!
My God!
Why have you forsaken me?
I am poured out like water
And my tongue sticks to the roof of my mouth.
They have pierced my hands and my feet
And cast lots for my clothing.
O my God!
Why have you forsaken me?

NARRATOR: Jesus cried out again in a loud voice, and died. And the temple curtain was torn in two from top to bottom.

[*Pause. JESUS is slowly taken down from the cross.*]

Jesus was sacrificed once, to take away the sins of many people. We may now enter the very presence of God, because of the blood of Jesus shed for us. This is the life-giving way, opened to us by Christ, whose body was broken and torn apart for our forgiveness, our healing, and our reconciliation.

[*CHORUS holds hands, gathered around the dead body of JESUS.*]

*Tim Mayfield*

# 19 Nailed!

## THEME

The crucifixion was the place where Jesus was totally victorious over Satan.

## CAST AND COSTUME

SATAN, the Prince of darkness himself, immensely self-satisfied with himself, but playing it cool. He should be dressed as flamboyantly as possible, with a cloak, and carry a big Bible.

WOODWORM, a small insignificant demon, enthusiastically sycophantic. Any costume that suggests the hosts of hell. He should carry a very small Bible.

## SCRIPT

[*Enter WOODWORM followed by SATAN. They have just witnessed the crucifixion.*]

WOODWORM: [*Performing victory dance.*] We got 'im, we got 'im, we got 'im. Yeah! We got 'im, we got 'im, we got 'im. Yeah! That was *wicked*, Boss! That has to have been the baddest bit of business in the history of the world. Walked right into it, didn't he? Right into it, with his eyes wide open, and we nailed 'im! [*Mimes crucifix position.*] Bang! Bang!

SATAN: Yes. One of my better efforts, even though I say so myself.

WOODWORM: It was genius, Boss, sheer genius. That robe they put on him. And a reed for a sceptre. And then the wonderful whip.

SATAN: And the crown of thorns? A witty touch?

WOODWORM: Pure poetry.

SATAN: And where were this pathetic king's feeble followers?

WOODWORM: Scarpered! Every last one of them! Oh, apart from a few women. And that John character.

SATAN: [*Not wishing to dwell on this.*] But the crowning glory of the masterwork? The touch of real artistry? The best bit of the whole lot?

WOODWORM: The nails! The beautiful sound of metal crunching into flesh and bone and sinew. God's Son being torn apart by a world that he had made! [*Looks for confirmation.*] No?

SATAN: No. The best bit was, 'My God, my God, why have you left me?'

WOODWORM: Yeah? [*Baffled.*] Er, why?

SATAN: Idiot! Don't you see? Because he was dying, because he was suffering what they've all suffered ever since Adam; God had to abandon him, because God can't die. So the creature belongs to *me*!

WOODWORM: Does that mean he's coming here?

SATAN: As my prisoner. And it's even better than that. [*Ecstatic.*] You see, God knew it was going to happen!

WOODWORM: Eh?

SATAN: It's all here... in his book! [*Finds page.*] Listen, 'My God, my God, why hast thou forsaken me?' He knew, and still he let it happen!

WOODWORM: Er, he knew? I mean... actually predicted it?

SATAN: Yes! That's the best bit.
[*Pause.*]

WOODWORM: But erm... Boss...

SATAN: Yes?

WOODWORM: He's God, right? So if he said it was going to happen, doesn't that mean he wanted it to happen? For some reason?

SATAN: [*Icily sarcastic.*] And what reason would that be?

WOODWORM: Oh... I just thought I... somewhere in Isaiah.... [*Gets out small Bible, reads under breath and finally attempts to conceal book from SATAN.*]

SATAN: What? Give me that! [*Snatches book and reads. Long pause.*] Oh.

WOODWORM: You know what this means, Boss? We haven't nailed him. He's nailed us.

*Barbara Sumner*

# 20 Heaven's Above

## THEME

The amazing grace of God, with special reference to the penitent thief (Lk 23:40–3). Though the setting is heaven, the sketch is not meant to be a theological statement about that place, but rather a fun sketch to make people think.

## CAST

MARTIN, who has died only a few moments before sketch opens; the ANGEL assigned to show him around—he is very polite and efficient and carries a clipboard; CATHY a very punky girl who has also recently entered heaven.

## COSTUMES

Left to the producer's imagination, apart from the clipboard!

## SCRIPT

MARTIN: Wow! [*Looking around him.*]
ANGEL: It is very beautiful, isn't it, sir?
MARTIN: This place is out of this world.
ANGEL: Precisely.
MARTIN: Gold, emeralds, and that amazing singing. They'll never listen to me in the PCC when I try to tell 'em about this lot.
ANGEL: I'm afraid you're absolutely right there, sir, they won't. I'm afraid you won't be telling them anything at all, sir. Not for quite a while. Although, I think some of them are due *here* a lot sooner than they think. [*He checks his file.*]
MARTIN: What?
ANGEL: You've passed over, sir.
MARTIN: [*Looks down at shoes.*] Passed over what?
ANGEL: From death to life, sir.
MARTIN: You mean...this is really heaven. Wow!
ANGEL: That would rather sum it up, sir, yes.

MARTIN: And all these people.

ANGEL: Yes, sir, they are the souls that have gone before.

MARTIN: Gone before what?

ANGEL: You, sir.

MARTIN: Oh. Why have they all got marks on their faces?

ANGEL: Foreheads, sir, to be precise. That is the seal of God. They belong to him now.

MARTIN: Then.... [*Points to forehead.*]

ANGEL: That's right, sir. You too. If you'd like to join this queue.

MARTIN: Sure. Anything. This place is so beautiful.

[*He stands behind a scruffy female.*]

CATHY: Whatcha, guv.

MARTIN: Wha... I'm sorry, were you talking to me?

CATHY: Yeah. [*Chewing gum.*] I said, watcha, how ya doing?

MARTIN: Well, apart from passing over from death to life—I'm fine.

CATHY: Right, yeah. I know the feeling. [*Spits.*]

[*MARTIN is horrified, and glances to ANGEL who smiles back and nods.*]

CATHY: What you up here for then, eh? I'm a druggie me. Ya know, the hard stuff.... 'Fraid it got me in the end. How about you?

MARTIN: *What?!* I mean... what?

CATHY: Yeah, I know, whotta waste o' talent, eh?

MARTIN: [*Aside to ANGEL.*] Excuse me. But I think she's in the wrong place.

ANGEL: [*Who has been studying his notes.*] Hmmm?

MARTIN: I said—I think she's got the wrong place.

[*Both look at CATHY who spits again, then grins, still chewing.*]

MARTIN: I think she should be.... [*points downwards.*]

ANGEL: No, sir. We don't make mistakes here.

MARTIN: But....

ANGEL: Have you ever heard of Billy Graham, sir?

MARTIN: Of course I have. In fact, I had the privilege of being led to the Lord by him.

CATHY: Oh, right. [*Punches him.*] Join the club. He got me an' all. It's a small world, eh?

MARTIN: Apparently, yes. [*With distaste.*]

CATHY: See him over there? [*She points off stage.*]
[*MARTIN backs off to avoid contact with CATHY.*]

CATHY: He's a Billy G. job an' all. And he'd been down for armed robbery—twice. Second time he was innocent though.

MARTIN: Oh... second time? Very nice. [*To ANGEL, horrified.*] Armed robbery!?

ANGEL: I'm afraid so, sir. God's love *is* incredible, isn't it? Even us angels never cease to be amazed at who comes in here. You see that chap over there. Now you've got the room next to him.

MARTIN: Don't tell me, he's armed robbery as well, is he?

ANGEL: Oh no, no, sir. Not at all.

MARTIN: Thank goodness for that.

ANGEL: He's a murderer.

MARTIN: *What?* Look, are you sure I've got the right place. I mean, I....

ANGEL: Oh yes, we don't *make* any mistakes here, sir, everyone is here who should be.

MARTIN: Yes, but... *him*?

ANGEL: Oh, but that's no surprise. You'll have heard about him already.

MARTIN: Oh no, I won't. I can assure you I've got nothing to do with the likes of him. You've got that one wrong. You'd better check with the Boss over him. I bet there's an error there.

ANGEL: No need to, sir. He's here as a direct result of an encounter with the Lord Jesus.

MARTIN: You mean... he's met Jesus?

ANGEL: Oh yes. A long time ago—on a cross. They died together, it's quite a story. You see, sir, like I said, we don't *make* mistakes up here, we just take them in.

*Dave Hopwood*

## 21 Jesus is Back

THEME

The Resurrection.

CAST

JOURNALIST, FISHERMAN.

COSTUME

Either biblical dress, modern dress or T-shirts and jeans.

PROPS

Table and items on it to suggest a newspaper journalist's desk.

SCRIPT

JOURNALIST: [*On phone at a desk.*] Look, I'm a reporter. Of course I've heard the rumours—that's why I'm calling you. I knew you'd have both ears to the ground...well, you know what I mean. So what have you got?...Yeah...Yeah... that's what I like to hear...No, of course I didn't believe the rumours...I just like to get the word from grass roots level, you know—what the people are saying.... Right, so you'll get in touch when you hear where they've hidden the body.... [*Laughs.*] Yeah, it's not only how do you lose a corpse, but it's a case of where to look when you've lost one...embarrassing. [*Going quiet to allow attention to go to FISHERMAN entering.*] Hey, tell me, how's that Barabbus research coming on?

FISHERMAN: [*Rushing in.*] I want to speak to someone on the Jesus case.

JOURNALIST: [*To FISHERMAN.*] Yes? [*To phone.*] No, I am listening....

FISHERMAN: Are you doing the Jesus story?

JOURNALIST: [*To FISHERMAN.*] Yes...who wants to know?

FISHERMAN: I do!

JOURNALIST: Obviously...[*To phone.*] Hang on a sec. [*To FISHERMAN.*] Well you'll have to hang on, this is important. [*To phone.*] Sorry about that....

FISHERMAN: The rumours are true. Jesus is back.

JOURNALIST: [*To FISHERMAN.*] Oh, give me a break.... [*To phone.*] What? Not you. No, honestly, I'm *not* getting funny with you. There's this fisherman in the office. Yes, of course I'm sure, [*whispering*]. I can smell him!

FISHERMAN: Will you listen to me, Jesus is alive and well. He spoke to me.

JOURNALIST: [*To phone.*] He spoke to him...to Jesus. I'll ask him. [*To FISHERMAN.*] Are you all right?

FISHERMAN: Yes, I'm all right.

JOURNALIST: [*To phone.*] He's all right.... No, not *Jesus* is all right, *he's* all right.

FISHERMAN: Yes, that's what I'm saying; Jesus is all right.

JOURNALIST: [*To phone.*] *And* Jesus is all right. They're both all right, all right?

FISHERMAN: About thirty of us have seen him so far.

JOURNALIST: [*To phone.*] There're about thirty of them.... No, not in the office. About thirty of them have seen him. [*To FISHERMAN.*] And they're all all right? [*To phone.*] Don't start that again. [*To FISHERMAN.*] He doesn't believe you.

FISHERMAN: [*Loudly.*] Well, if he's not dead, who's got the body then?

JOURNALIST: [*To phone.*] D'you hear that? [*To FISHERMAN.*] Obviously, the Romans.

FISHERMAN: [*Sarcasticly.*] Funny, I don't see them parading it round the streets.

JOURNALIST: [*To phone.*] Uhuh, any other offers? [*To FISHERMAN.*] The priests maybe?

FISHERMAN: Ask him if the priests had it; doesn't he think they'd produce it and stop the rumours?

JOURNALIST: [*To FISHERMAN.*] Absolutely. [*To phone.*]

Wouldn't they produce the body? [*To FISHERMAN.*] Unless the disciples stole the body.

FISHERMAN: What about the guards?

JOURNALIST: [*To FISHERMAN.*] What about the guards? Ah [*to phone*], what about the guards? [to FISHERMAN.] No. No they wouldn't have it.

FISHERMAN: No. I mean how did a bunch of civilians get past the crack temple guards at the tomb?

JOURNALIST: [*To FISHERMAN.*] You're good at this aren't you? [*To phone.*] Ready for this one? How did they steal the body when the guards were there? [*Timidly.*] They were asleep?

FISHERMAN: Is he serious?

JOURNALIST: [*To phone.*] Are you serious? [*To FISHERMAN, having been shouted at.*] He's serious.

FISHERMAN: Well ask your friend this: is the tomb empty?

JOURNALIST: [*To phone.*] Is the tomb empty? [*To FISHERMAN.*] Of course it's empty.

FISHERMAN: Well tell your friend to face the facts.

JOURNALIST: [*To phone.*] Face the facts.

FISHERMAN: And tell him he can't ignore the evidence.

JOURNALIST: [*To phone.*] You can't ignore the evidence.

FISHERMAN: Tell him.... No, I'll tell him. Call back when you get some sort of argument together.... Hello?... [*To JOURNALIST.*] He hung up!

*Trapdoor Theatre Company*

# 22 Sherlock Holmes Investigates… The Case of the Missing Corpse

## THEME

The Resurrection.

## CAST

DR WATSON—Bumbling and a bit thick.
SHERLOCK HOLMES—The super-sleuth.
DISCIPLE—Just a loud voice—he does not appear on stage.
LANDLADY—A bit of a dragon.
SOLDIER—Officer type.
BURGLAR—Shifty type.

## COSTUME AND PROPS

DR WATSON has notebook and pencils in trouser pocket, but with a large audience he should write on a big board or overhead projector.
SHERLOCK HOLMES wears cloak and deerstalker hat. Needs pipe and magnifying glass. Both SHERLOCK HOLMES and DR WATSON need identity cards. If the audience is large, these should be huge pieces of card with very big lettering.
SOLDIER wears uniform and beret.
BURGLAR wears black eye-mask.

## STAGING

Each 'scene' should take place in a different area of the acting space. The final scene needs the 'grave-clothes' (perhaps a sheet and pillowcase) laid on a table or bench.

## SCRIPT

[*As the sketch starts, WATSON and HOLMES enter or are already on stage.*]

WATSON: The strangest investigation it was ever my privilege to witness was the Case of the Missing Corpse. My friend Sherlock Holmes received a call from the highest authority in the land, who gave him only a few hours to solve the mystery.

HOLMES: [*Sucking at his pipe.*] Watson, I perceive you have a notebook and pencil in your lefthand trouser pocket.

WATSON: Good heavens, Holmes! How on earth...?
[*He produces book and pencil from the pocket.*]

HOLMES: You know my methods, Watson. Now write down the names of the suspects, so we can eliminate them one by one and work out who moved the body of Jesus.

WATSON: [*As he writes.*] Who moved Jesus' body?

HOLMES: There are Jesus' disciples or followers—they might have moved him to bury him nearer home.

WATSON: [*Writing.*] Disciples.

HOLMES: Or the government—they may have taken the corpse to stop a riot, or block any plans to build a church on the spot later.

WATSON: [*Writing.*] Government.

HOLMES: Or burglars.

WATSON: Burglars? [*He tries twice to spell it right, crosses it out and puts 'theeves' instead.*]

HOLMES: Burglars, Watson. Jesus was buried in the cemetery of a very rich man. Robbers do sometimes loot these graves to see what they can get. That's all.

WATSON: All?

HOLMES: Three suspects, Watson. No more.

WATSON: Only three?

HOLMES: Only three. No one else could have the slightest interest in the corpse of Jesus of Nazareth. The question is, which of the three moved the corpse?
[*They move to a corner of the stage.*]

WATSON: First of all, we tracked down the hideout of Jesus' disciples. They were under cover in an attic flat in Jerusalem. I knocked on the door. [*Mimes.*] There was no answer. I tried the handle, but it was locked. [*Mimes.*]

DISCIPLE: [*Off.*] Who's that?

WATSON: Dr Watson.
DISCIPLE: Dr Who?
WATSON: Open up...in the name of—Sherlock Holmes!
DISCIPLE: [*Pause.*] Who's he?
[*Enter LANDLADY.*]
LANDLADY: What's all this noise?
WATSON: Madam, we wish to speak to the disciples of Jesus.
LANDLADY: Well, you can't. They've locked themselves in. Won't come out for anyone, not now that Jesus is dead.
HOLMES: How long have they been in there?
LANDLADY: Since Friday night. Haven't set a foot outside since. Scared to death, they are. [*Exit.*]
WATSON: Wait a minute, Holmes. [*Excited.*] That means they can't have done it. If they've been in here for thirty-six hours.
HOLMES: My dear Watson, that much was already obvious. The government has an armed guard round the graveyard. How could these eleven or twelve disciples and a few women have given them the slip and broken through?
WATSON: [*Deflated.*] Oh.
HOLMES: It's out of the question.
WATSON: Oh. Not the disciples, then. [*He crosses them off his list.*] Well, how about that armed guard and the government?
HOLMES: Better, Watson. You're improving.
WATSON: Ah, now we're on to something!
[*They move to another corner of the stage.*]
WATSON: We called at the governor's palace and sent in our identity cards. [*SOLDIER collects them and takes them off stage.*] But all that came out was the soldier who had been commanding the company set on guard on Friday night.
[*Enter SOLDIER.*]
HOLMES: Have you taken custody of the corpse of Jesus?
SOLDIER: Indeed we have not. We wish we had.
WATSON: Really, why?
SOLDIER: *If* we had got the body we would put it on display at once to stop all this fuss. We're not

getting a moment's peace from the press and television people. The facts of the matter are simply these. During Saturday night there was a thunderstorm and earth tremor. The tombstone came unstuck and got dislodged. At first light this morning, we found the grave broken into and the body stolen.

HOLMES: [*Pouncing at once.*] Stolen?

[*SOLDIER salutes and exit.*]

WATSON: [*Getting there more slowly.*] Ah, *stolen*! So, Holmes, if it wasn't the government [*crosses them off his list*] then it was burglars who *stole* the body. Holmes, we've solved it!

HOLMES: Come on, Watson. No time to lose.

[*They move to back of stage.*]

WATSON: We looked up one of Holmes' contacts in the underworld.

[*Enter BURGLAR, furtively.*]

Name of...

HOLMES and BURGLAR: [*Together, anxiously.*] Watson?

WATSON: [*Misunderstanding.*] Really, I never knew that. [*Advancing to shake hands.*] My dear fellow, Watson's my name too. Delighted to meet...

[*BURGLAR retreats.*]

HOLMES: Watson, no *names* please. He's wanted by the police.

WATSON: Oh, I see. [*He clearly doesn't.*]

HOLMES: [*Turns back to BURGLAR.*] Now we need your inside knowledge. Which gang would have done this?

BURGLAR: Which of 'em? None of 'em. You can see a mile off it's not a burglar's job. When we do in a grave, we take the clothes the body's wrapped in. They're worth a bit of money. But we leave the rotten old corpse behind. Nobody wants that.

HOLMES: Whereas in this case...

BURGLAR: 'Sright. They've nicked the corpse but left the clothes.

WATSON: By Jove, Holmes, that's true. The clothes were still there in the grave.

[*BURGLAR takes fright at WATSON's loud voice and exit.*]

WATSON: [*Bewildered.*] But Holmes, if it wasn't the burglars [*crosses them off the list*] and it wasn't the government and it wasn't the disciples, who was it? The corpse couldn't have moved itself, could it?

HOLMES: [*Suddenly seeing the light.*] Watson, you're a genius!

WATSON: [*Smiles, very pleased.*] Oh, my dear fellow. [*Realises he doesn't know why; looks mystified.*] But I mean to say....

HOLMES: Quick, Watson! Why didn't I see it before? We may be too late.

WATSON: Too late? But what....

HOLMES: Come *on*. Those grave-clothes.

WATSON: Grave-clothes?

HOLMES: Yes, they're wrong.

WATSON: [*Following feebly.*] The wrong grave-clothes...?

[*They race to where the grave-clothes are laid. HOLMES examines them closely with his magnifying glass.*]

HOLMES: Just as I thought. Not a finger-print anywhere. No trace of anyone disturbing them. They are lying *exactly* as they did when the body was inside.

WATSON: So....

HOLMES: So the only possible explanation is that the body somehow evaporated through them and then out of the grave.

WATSON: Evaporated...?

HOLMES: In other words, Jesus is not dead anymore, but he has come back to life in a new way.

WATSON: Back to life...oh *really*, Holmes!

HOLMES: Yes, *really*, Watson. Rule out the impossible and whatever you have left, however improbable, is the truth. I think you will find that if you call on Jesus now, he is here...alive.

WATSON: [*Half repeating, half trying it out.*] Jesus... alive...here?

[*They look round, freeze and then exit.*]

*Lance Pierson*

# 23 I'll Soon Wipe That Scowl off Tommy's Face

THEME

Easter, Jesus' resurrection, or doubts.

CAST

Two actors, who simply follow the words and actions from Fig. 10 to Fig. 19. BARNABUS should carry brush and paints; THOMAS should stand behind or hold a picture-frame.

SCRIPT

This takes the form of a cartoon from the book *The Gospel According to Barnabas* (Kevin Mayhew Ltd, 1975) by Graham Jeffery. The author has very kindly agreed to it being used in this way.

I'LL SOON WIPE THAT SCOWL OF TOMMY'S FACE

Figure 10

ONE SURE STROKE OF MY BRUSH AND THAT LOOK OF SORROW WILL BECOME A SMILE OF HAPPINESS AND PEACE

Figure 11

FOR THOUGH JESUS REALLY WAS CRUCIFIED, NOW HE IS ALIVE AND WELL

Figure 12

AND MARY HAS SEEN HIM,
AND PETER HAS SEEN HIM

Figure 13

AND BECAUSE JESUS IS ALIVE,
WE SHALL LIVE ALSO

Figure 14

NOT JUST ON THIS PLANET FOR A
FEW SCORE YEARS AND TEN

Figure 15

BUT IN HEAVEN WITH JESUS
FOR EVER AND EVER

Figure 16

SO PLEASE SMILE, THOMAS

Figure 17

Figure 18

WITH A STORY LIKE THAT,
YOU DON'T NEED A PAINT BRUSH

Figure 19

# 24 A Farewell Present

## THEME

The promise of the Holy Spirit based on Acts 1.

## CAST

Three of Jesus' disciples walking back to Jerusalem after Jesus has been taken up into heaven. Each is slightly confused and trying to make sense of the promise Jesus left with them.

## COSTUME AND PROPS

Modern casual wear will help the audience see this is as relevant today as in biblical times.

## SCRIPT

[*Enter 1, 2 and 3, if possible from the back of the church, walking slowly towards the front.*]

1: So now what?
2: Eh?
1: What do we do now?
3: You heard him, go back to Jerusalem.
1: Of course I heard him, I'm not deaf. I just didn't understand that other bit.
2: What the, 'wait for the gift my Father promised'?
1: Yeah. I mean I remember him talking about the... you know.
3: Holy Spirit?
1: Yeah, but I've never really understood it.
2: He always did have a funny way of saying things. How can you get baptised in spirit?
3: Perhaps it's another story; he always told good stories.
1: It's another of those stories that mean something else?
2: Yes, something is going to happen to us that's like John's baptism in water.
1: Instead of going under the water you get soaked by Holy Spirit! [*Pause.*] It doesn't make much sense to me.

3: A lot of things didn't make much sense. His death for example. I didn't understand how that could have happened.
2: And seeing him again, alive and well, now that's not normal! After he explained it though, it all seemed to click.
1: So this baptism in the Holy Spirit will make sense when we get to it?
2: Sure, anyway we're never going to really understand it until we've experienced it first hand.
3: Ah, but we do know it's going to be powerful. Anything that's going to make this lazy bones get out there witnessing to people has to be powerful!
1: To the ends of the earth! That's a long way. How are we few going to cover all that ground? It would take several lifetimes.
3: You saw what happened when the Boss spoke: crowds started following us and when they went home they couldn't stop telling people.
1: That's true.
2: Yeah, but he's the Son of God. I'm nothing but a fisherman.
3: Don't you see? That must be it.
2: What?
1: Yeah, what?
3: This Holy Spirit is going to be like having Jesus with us. It's going to help us be like Jesus. His power.
2: His words.
1: His witnesses.
2: And that's all for us?
1: All who wait for it.

*Colin Mengell*

# 25 Holy Spirit—Who Are You?

## THEME

To illustrate five characteristics of the Holy Spirit.

## CAST

Two narrators, who stand either side of the action, and three people to form freeze frames. These mimers should form a three-person shape to indicate the Three Persons of the Trinity and they should return to this form for each new stanza. They will need to work out carefully beforehand suitable mime positions for the five characteristics.

## COSTUME

Jeans and T-shirts.

## SCRIPT

NARRATOR 1: God is Father, Son and Holy Spirit, but....
Holy Spirit—who are you? Where are you? What are you?

NARRATOR 2: I am the Spirit of Jesus at work on this earth—
I'll remind you what he's like and help you be more like him.
[*Mime: eg, one person showing another what a third is doing.*]

NARRATOR 1: God is Father, Son and Holy Spirit, but....
Holy Spirit—who are you? Where are you? What are you?

NARRATOR 2: I am the Spirit of wisdom and understanding—I know what's on your heart, the concerns that sometimes weigh you down; Tell me, I want to help.
[*Mime: eg, one person bends to form a chair, the second sits with head down, the third crouches in front to look encouragingly into his/her face.*]

NARRATOR 1: God is Father, Son and Holy Spirit, but....

Holy Spirit—who are you? Where are you? What are you?

NARRATOR 2: I am God's miracle worker—the unseen agent at work to bring about God's purposes and to reveal God's glory.

[*Mime: eg, two stand together as if holding a baby, while the third (unnoticed by the two) crouching symbolically holds up the baby.*]

NARRATOR 1: God is Father, Son and Holy Spirit, but....
Holy Spirit—who are you? Where are you? What are you?

NARRATOR 2: I am energy for life—giving you resources you never dreamed you had.

[*Mime: eg, side-view of two in a running race, one slightly ahead because of the pushing force of the third.*]

NARRATOR 1: God is Father, Son and Holy Spirit, but....
Holy Spirit—who are you? Where are you? What are you?

NARRATOR 2: I am your companion—always at your side, wanting to be your very best friend.

[*Mime: eg, two with heads bowed, hands clasped as if in prayer, a third with his hand resting on their shoulders.*]

*Pete Chantry*

# 26 Climbing

## THEME

We cannot live the Christian life to the full unless we use the gifts that the Holy Spirit provides. Based on 1 Corinthians 12.

## CAST

NARRATOR.
DAVID (very self-confident, but truly loves God).
SHOPKEEPER.
MOUNTAINEER.

## COSTUME AND PROPS

A plain covered book and simple climbing equipment such as a rope and hammer.
NARRATOR—can wear black.
DAVID—dressed in casual clothes unsuitable for a climb.
SHOPKEEPER—wears a caretaker's jacket.
MOUNTAINEER—wears clothes suitable for climbing, and carries climbing equipment.

## SCRIPT

NARRATOR speaks throughout

There once was a man called David, who felt God wanted him to climb to the top of a nearby mountain.

[*Enter DAVID who looks up the mountain.*]

He was so sure about this call from God that he bought himself a mountaineering book.

[*Enter SHOPKEEPER who sells him the book.*]
[*DAVID starts reading it as the SHOPKEEPER exits.*]

It had all you needed to know about climbing mountains, even where to get your kit from. David read the book very carefully, but when he got to the chapter on equipment he didn't understand all the technical names so he skipped a few passages until he got to the first steps of climbing.

[*DAVID slowly reads, thinking over each piece of information, and then shrugs his shoulders and quickly turns a few pages.*]

'This is more like it,' thought David. 'Let's get to it.' And with that he sets off to the foot of the mountain.

[*Starts to walk (front mime walk if possible).*]

Up the sloping foothills he walked, feeling quite pleased with his progress. Things were going well—after all, he had the book to follow. He knew he could put his faith in it because it had passages explaining what experienced mountaineers had learnt.

[*DAVID holds the book close to his heart, giving it a little pat.*]

The sloping foothills began to get steeper, and David referred to the book to check on his progress.

[*Reads the book while putting more effort into the walk.*]

Yes, all was going well. He knew the best way to proceed and he felt closer to God with each step he took. Soon he came to a rock-face where a mountaineer was preparing his equipment for the climb ahead.

[*Enter MOUNTAINEER.*]

David politely greeted this fellow-climber as he passed by and started to climb.

[*DAVID waves and starts to climb. The MOUNTAINEER looks surprised but waves back.*]

The mountaineer was surprised by this encounter in the middle of nowhere, but was even more surprised to see that David didn't have any equipment with him. Calling out to David he asked why he didn't have any. David called back, explaining that he didn't need equipment because he had the book. 'But wait!' the mountaineer tried to call up, but David just kept on climbing.

[*Exit the MOUNTAINEER.*]

Upwards and onwards David kept going, admiring the view as he went. The rock-face got steeper and the handholds got fewer.

[*Slowly, with much more effort, DAVID keeps climbing.*]

Higher and higher he went until there were hardly any cracks or ridges to step onto. At this point the view didn't look so lovely, it had taken on a much more worrying appearance. David kept on reading the book, trying to work out what to do next, but all the book referred to was some technical equipment he didn't have.

[*Reads with difficulty as he is hanging on, and scratches his head.*]

Onwards he went, up and up, until finally he came to solid rock with no footholds at all.

[*DAVID stops, searches, but doesn't find a hold.*]

He checked the book, but again all it talked about was using some strange equipment, and so with sadness he had to admit he could go no further. He decided to turn back, but on trying to climb down the rock-edge broke away from under him and he had to pull himself back up.

[*Slips, but pulls himself up to the next ledge.*]

What was he to do? He couldn't go up and he could no longer climb down. He was stuck. Why oh why had God led him to this point?

[*DAVID looks up to heaven.*]

He was very scared and cried out to God to save him.

[*Enter MOUNTAINEER.*]

Below, coming up slower but much more safely was the mountaineer, who heard David crying out to God and called up to him. David was so pleased to see the mountaineer and thanked God for his rescue. The mountaineer climbed up and threw a rope over for David to tie around himself. Then by using his equipment he chipped handholds out of the cracks in the rock and fixed pegs for footholds. Slowly the two climbed up until they teached a big ridge where they rested.

'I hope this teaches you a lesson,' said the mountaineer. 'Never attempt a climb without the right equipment. It's all in that book you've got.' And they went through the book again with the mountaineer explaining what each piece of equipment was and how to use it.

[*The two continue to read the book.*]

David learnt a lesson about climbing, but like him, each of us are called to do something. As Christians we're all called to live a life that's pleasing to God but how many of us try to do so without the equipment the Holy Spirit provides?

*Colin Mengell*

# 27 The House With Three Owners

## THEME

To illustrate the Trinity.

## CAST

Speaker (S).
Preferably three boys of about nine years old (1, 2 and 3) who should overact considerably and mime all the gestures that S describes.

## COSTUMES AND PROPS

Casual clothes or jeans and T-shirts. The props should be as indicated in the script.

## SCRIPT

S: There was this house—a vast great hall—well, a bit of a barn, really. One day a man came along and said:
1: This is my house.
S: And he folded his arms and looked pleased with himself. But just then another man came along and said:
2: This is *my* house.
S: And he winked his eye, and folded his arms and looked pleased with himself. When, would you believe, another man came along and said:
3: This is *my* house.
S: And he stamped his foot and winked his eye and folded his arms and looked pleased with himself. Meanwhile the first man was no longer looking pleased at all.
1: I said it's my house.
S: At which the second man said:
2: Mine, you mean.
S: And the third said:
3: Not at all, it's mine.
1: Mine
2: Mine

3: Mine

ALL 3: [*Deep breath.*] Mine!

S: And they came to blows.

[*1 and 3 assault each other, knocking 2—and each other—to the ground in the process.*]

The first man picked himself up and complained:

1: But it *is* mine. I built it. [*He produces a brick.*]

S: The second man picked himself up, dusted himself down and complained:

2: But it *is* mine. I bought it. [*He produces a £5 note.*]

S: The third man picked himself up, dusted himself down, pulled himself together and complained:

3: But it *is* mine. I live in it. [*He produces a key.*]

ALL 3: [*Deep breath.*] Ohhhh! So it *is* yours as well as mine.

[*They walk off arm-in-arm.*]

*Optional ending:*

S: And in the same way, we belong to God three times over. God the Father made us. Jesus, God the Son, paid for us by dying the death our sins deserved on the cross. And God the Holy Spirit lives in us; he shouldn't be just a lodger, but our owner-occupier.

*Lance Pierson*

# 28 The Jam Factory

## THEME

This sketch is an attempt to retell the well-known parable of the sower (Mt 13:3–23) in terms which might be more accessible to people who live in the city, where farmers chucking seed on the ground are somewhat rare. The overtones of the dialect used here are deliberately Scouse. You could obviously 'translate' the story again into whatever local dialect is most suitable for your performance.

## CAST

This sketch was originally performed as a 'group narration'. One strong central narrator, supported by a group of actors, all shapes and sizes, who illustrate the story with vigorous choreographed actions and punctuate it with sound effects or other vocal reactions. The most obvious places for action and sound effects (SFX) within the script are indicated with instructions in brackets. There will be many other possibilities which emerge during your rehearsals, use these as a guide. The group should spend some time developing the actions, noises and production-line movements of a modern factory—the crazier, the better.

## COSTUMES

T-shirts and jeans.

## SCRIPT

NARRATOR: Hey, you lot! Will you stop dozin' and wake up!

[*The group rouse themselves grumpily. The NARRATOR addresses the audience.*]

I'm gonna tell yous a story an' it's dead good. So shurrup an' get them ears pinned right back. [*action.*] There was this factory, like, and it was a biggun, OK, a great biggun and guess what they made there? [*Various suggestions.*] Jam. You know, for jam butties, tarts, rolls, cakes. [*Voice: Did they make traffic jams there?*] Shurrup, you. Now in dis factory there were all these machines, like, sweatin' and puffin' [*SFX/action*], whirrin' and chuffin' [*SFX/action*], spittin' and coughin' [*SFX/action*]. And these four crates of strawberries got loaded onto a fork-lift truck, which was for loadin' crates not forks, right? And there was this divvy, you know, a thicko, drivin' it [*action*] and coming the other way there was another thicko, you know, a divvy, drivin' backwards in the opposite direction [*action*]. And they crashed [*SFX/action*]. One crate fell off and all them little strawberries started runnin' all over [*panicky little voices*]. But they needn't have worried, 'cos there was this sockin' great steam-roller comin' round the corner [*SFX/action*]. Pulped 'em flat [*SFX*], pressed into the tarmac. And that was the end of the first crate.

[*Voice: Worrabout the other three crates?*]

I'm comin' to them. The second crate gorra bit further. They went through the washers [*action/ SFX*]. Got stuffed down this machine that pulled their tops off [*shrieks*] and they were going great—they actually made it to the sugar an' the syrup! But some bozo stuck a great spanner in the fuse-box. 'E wanted a break for 'is cuppa, and everything went [*SFX: bang!*]. And some bloke lit a fag and it went [*SFX: bang!*] again. Think of all them strawberries, baked, done to a turn. Only that's the trouble, you couldn' turn 'em—stuck hard they were [*Voice: Tough, eh?*] Very tough. As tough as a rhino's toenails, in fact. So that was the end of the second crate.

But the *third* crate did even better, it actually got boiled up with sugar and that, you know—bubblin' [*SFX/action*] and hissin' [*SFX*] and it was like...er...well...it was like strawberry jam being boiled up. A flippin' great vat-full. A million butties worth of jam and you know what happened? A million wasps came thro' the window [*SFX/action*] and they all got stuck in. Because some totally incompetent person had left the lid off. [*Voice: Sorry wack!*] And he was sorry, because he got stung about nine million times. Anyway, the manager tried to sell it as waspberry jam, but it didn't catch on. So that was the end of the third crate.

VOICE: So that just leaves the fourth crate.

2ND VOICE: When did you learn to count to four?

VOICE: Shurrup you, or I'll burst yer.

3RD VOICE: What was wrong with that crate, then?

NARRATOR: Nothing, it was perfect. I suppose you can call jam perfect. It was good jam—cracker. It got the whole works. Washed [*SFX/action for each stage of this production line*] snipped, sweetened, boiled, packed and sealed.

VOICE: Did it get walrussed as well as sealed?

NARRATOR: I think I'll ignore that, if you don't mind. It was totally processed and came out in great red dollops, all over bits of toast, butties, cakes, bibs, ties and tablecloths, just like normal jam. So the fourth crate was—[*Voice: The jammy one!*] Thank you. Yeah. It was the only one that made it to the toast.

VOICE: I propose a toast: The Fourth Crate.

ALL: The Fourth Crate!

NARRATOR: So the moral of the story, you know, the point, the purpose, like, is this: The first crate is like the divvys who hear God's word but don't do nothin' about it. They don't even get inside the factory—they fall off the truck and get squashed [*SFX*]. That second crate of strawberries is like them who hear God's good news and do something about it, but they don't stay plugged into the mains. Like they don't pray—never talk to God, worship him or do what he says. The power cut makes 'em go off the boil—hard and cold. The third crate is slightly different—like those who hear God's word and really get going great guns, bubbling away, you know, full of enthusiasm and stuff, but then troubles come, like them wasps, the cares of the world, like spendin' the whole time thinkin' how much money I'm getting and they get gummed up and thrown out. And that was the end of the third crate.

The fourth crate is like those people who hear God's word and actually get it together—stirred up, spread out and tasty!

ALL: Stirred up! Spread out! And tasty!

*Breadrock Theatre Company*

# 29 The Non-Hallowe'en Party

## THEME

A Christian alternative to the traditional and evil celebration of Hallowe'en.

## CAST

A boy, BARRY, and a girl, LINDA.

## COSTUME

Teenage dress.

## STAGING

The simplest items to suggest a suburban sitting-room. It may not be possible to erect a front door, but that part of the sketch could be easily mimed.

## SCRIPT

[*BARRY enters with a video, talking on a mobile phone.*]

BARRY: No, Mum and Dad have gone out tonight, and so they said I could get a video out. Want to come over? It's called *Werewolf Witch Meets the Voodoo Monster*. Well, I thought I'd get something scary 'cause it's Hallowe'en. Can't you come? Oh well, never mind. Yeah, probably see you tomorrow sometime. Bye.
[*Hangs up phone.*]
[*Reading video jacket.*] 'You'll be too scared to scream! Never before has a motion picture brought such horror into your home! Unthinkable evil, before your very eyes! See the Voodoo Monster as it takes on different personalities and entices children to their doom! Are you ready for this experience of terror? Light a candle and turn off all your lights.' [*He does so.*] 'Make sure that your door's locked tight before you turn on this

truly terrifying videotape! Because the worst thing is, it could happen to you!'
[*As he locks the door, he hears a knocking sound. He jumps out of skin.*] What was that? Oh, it was the front door. [*nervously.*] Hello? Who's there?

LINDA: [*Off.*] Barry! It's me!

BARRY: Who?

LINDA: [*Off.*] It's Linda from next door.

BARRY: Oh. Well, what do you want?

LINDA: [*Off.*] Can I come in for a second?

BARRY: [*A bit scared.*] Mum and Dad have gone out, see, and I'm not supposed to let anyone in really.

LINDA: I don't think they'd mind if you let *me* in, Barry.

BARRY: [*Muttering to himself.*] Yes, if it's really you. But what if you're the Voodoo Monster in disguise?

LINDA: [*Off.*] What did you say, Barry?

BARRY: Nothing, I'll just unlock the door now.

LINDA: [*Stepping in.*] Thanks, Barry. What's the matter?

BARRY: [*He has been staring at her.*] Nothing, I just....

LINDA: Why are you sitting here in the dark? Have you had a power cut? [*Turning on the light and seeing the video.*] Oh, you haven't been spooking yourself with one of these scary videos, have you?

BARRY: No, I haven't started watching it yet. Anyway, I like scary videos. And it's Hallowe'en. You know, witches and vampires and werewolves and things.

LINDA: Hallowe'en's the American name. We call it All Hallows' Eve at our church.

BARRY: Why?

LINDA: 'Cos it's the night before something, like Christmas Eve.

BARRY: What's it the night before?

LINDA: All Saints' Day, when we remember all God's holy people, and the saints like Matthew, Mark, Luke and John, St Paul, St Francis and Mother Teresa.

BARRY: Holy people and saints? They're OK for church people, but they sound a bit boring to me.

LINDA: I can promise you they're not. Joseph and his amazing dreamcoat? David and Goliath? But why don't you find out for yourself? That's why I came over—to invite you to our non-Hallowe'en party next door.

BARRY: How can you have a *non*-Hallowe'en party?

LINDA: Well, what's the point of celebrating ghosts and ghouls and witches and vampires? Actually, I don't believe in ghosts, but if any of those other things exist, then they're evil. We'd rather celebrate things that are *good*! Wouldn't you?

BARRY: Well, I suppose so.

LINDA: We're having a Praise Party! We're singing and dancing and playing games, and some of the kids are in fancy dress from the Bible, and it's really good fun!

BARRY: But I was going to watch the video. It's Hallowe'en....

LINDA: Well, it's up to you, Barry. I must say I'd rather be at a party, celebrating with my friends than sitting alone in the dark with a spooky old video. But stay here if you'd rather. Anyhow, we'd love to have you.

BARRY: [*To audience.*] What shall I do?

*Philip Glassborow*

# *B The Christian Life*

## 30 Getting Angry

THEME

The Cleansing of the Temple in Jerusalem: Matthew 21:12–13.

CAST AND COSTUME

There are two 'audiences': the main congregation or school watching the performance and the smaller audience of four people in modern informal dress KATE, DODO, and BAZ to whom STANLEY is telling the story.

SCRIPT

STANLEY: This is a story about getting angry.
DODO: About losing your temper.
STANLEY: No. About getting angry. There's a big difference.
DODO: Oh.
STANLEY: Imagine standing outside the biggest church you've ever seen.
BAZ: Westminster Abbey!
KATE: York Minster!
DODO: The Albert Hall!
KATE: Church, you goon.
STANLEY: The biggest ever church—a cathedral.
DODO: I'm not a goon.
STANLEY: And outside this cathedral there are thousands of people queuing to get in.
KATE: You are a goon.
DODO: I'm *not*!
STANLEY: Ssh. All these people are outside this cathedral queuing to get in, but they can't. Why?
DODO: Because they're too fat.
KATE: No, silly, they can't get in because the doors are locked.

DODO: I am *not* silly.
KATE: You are.
STANLEY: *Ssh!* Can we get on with this story?
KATE: [*Under her breath.*] Temper, temper.
STANLEY: LOOK, I CAN'T GO ON WITH THIS STORY UNLESS YOU KEEP QUIET!
BAZ: Go on then, a story about getting angry.
STANLEY: Yes, right. Where did I get to?
BAZ: This big church and all these people can't get in.
DODO: Well, that's pretty stupid, somebody should let them in.
STANLEY: They can't get in because they haven't got enough money.
BAZ: You mean they have to *pay* to get in?
STANLEY: Yes, they all have to go through a turnstile and buy a ticket for at least £1.50.
BAZ: Cor, what a rip off.
STANLEY: It gets worse—you have to pay to get in, *then* you have to pay £1 to hire a hymn book, £2 to sit down on a chair, £5 to say a prayer....
BAZ: I bet the vicar would be a millionaire. He'd have a private helicopter and a swimming pool.
KATE: An automatic sermon machine!
BAZ: A robot to teach in Sunday school!
STANLEY: But what would God think about people buying tickets to get into his house?
BAZ: He'd do his nut.
DODO: I bet he'd break down the doors and give them what for! Pow! Zap! Crunch!
STANLEY: That's just what *did* happen.
BAZ:
KATE: } What?
DODO:
STANLEY: Something very like that. It was when Jesus visited the Temple in Jerusalem where all the people would gather at Passover—the great feast. Jews and foreigners came from hundreds of miles just to be there. *But*...
BAZ: What?
STANLEY: It cost money. You had to pay the temple tax.
KATE: How much?

STANLEY: As much as £20. [*They draw in their breath.*] *And* you had to pay it in special money.

BAZ: Hm. Clever.

DODO: I don't see why that's clever.

STANLEY: Oh but it was, because if you turned up with Greek or Roman money you had to *change* it and the people who changed it for the special temple money made a fantastic profit giving you far less than your money was worth. And along with the money-changers, were people selling oxen and sheep and pigeons—you had to sacrifice them to God as part of your Passover offering and, of course, the people who sold them to you made a fat profit. Everybody in there—money-changers, pigeon-sellers, priests, were making a fat profit—except the ordinary people. They were making a fat loss!

KATE: A fat loss?

STANLEY: Well, you know what I mean. And more than that, it wasn't only all that swindling that Jesus saw right in the middle of God's house, it was noise—shouting, arguing, clattering of coins.

BAZ: Clatter, clatter!

STANLEY: Lowing of oxen.

KATE: Mooo!

STANLEY: Bleating of sheep.

DODO: Baaaa!

STANLEY: All together! [*They make the noises together.*] SILENCE! [*They stop.*] It was Jesus, so angry that nobody moved. He walked up to a table and on it was a pile of glittering silver coins. CRASH! He pushed it over. [*They gasp.*] CRASH! He pushed over another and another and another. There was no stopping him now. He took a rope and whipped the oxen and the sheep, who fled down the steps of the temple, followed by their owners, and he opened the cages of the pigeons and with a flurry of wings they were all soaring up into the sky. No one had ever seen Jesus angry like this before.

BAZ: Do you mean that sometimes you can be angry like that and it's OK with God?

STANLEY: Yes, but Jesus gave a reason for his anger. He said,

'God's house is a house of prayer, where everyone can come and talk to God, but *you* (he said to the people) have made it a den of robbers!'

KATE: [*Gasps.*] That was something to get angry about.

BAZ: Like paying five quid to say a prayer.

STANLEY: Yes.

DODO: Jesus didn't lose his temper, did he, Stanley?

STANLEY: I don't think so, no.

DODO: When I lose my temper I don't know what I'm doing, I just go AAAAH! and chuck things around.

STANLEY: That's the difference. Jesus knew exactly what he was doing. He was angry on purpose, not by accident. He was angry because he had thought a lot about God's house and wanted everybody to be able to come to God free of charge.

KATE: Is he still angry about it?

STANLEY: He is angry with anyone who tries to stop people talking to him.

*Breadrock Theatre Company*

# 31 Home Improvements

THEME

A parable of Christian conversion.

CAST

ANNE and DAVID, a young married couple.
RUTH, an old school friend of DAVID's.

COSTUME AND PROPS

Normal modern clothes and minimum props to suggest a lounge.

SCRIPT

DAVID: [*From kitchen.*] Milk and one sugar, was it, Ruth?
RUTH: No sugar, thanks, David. I've finally managed to give it up.
ANNE: Well done.
RUTH: It's lovely in here, Anne, but I can't say I've noticed any obvious changes since the last time.
DAVID: [*Entering with tray.*] Of course—it's the first time you've been since the conversion, isn't it? No, you're right. Perhaps the changes aren't immediately obvious.
RUTH: To be honest, I can't see any at all. But Anne said on the phone how pleased you both were.
ANNE: Oh yes. When we first heard about the offer it seemed a good idea, didn't it, Dave?
DAVID: Improved security; good investment for the future; that sort of thing.
ANNE: When the workmen actually got going, though, it turned out to be not quite what we'd expected!
DAVID: Gave us a thorough going-over.
RUTH: [*Puzzled.*] Oh. Didn't you complain?
ANNE: No, we were very pleased with the results.
RUTH: So...what exactly have you had done?
DAVID: Well, they started at the bottom—in the cellar, so to

speak. Cleaned out a lot of rubbish that had been there for ages; stuff we really didn't want to touch.

RUTH: [*Embarrassed.*] You don't have to... I mean, I didn't mean...

ANNE: That's all right. It's all part of the deal. All that had to be removed before the real structural changes could begin. That part has only just started.

RUTH: So they haven't finished yet?

DAVID: Oh no. As Anne says, we're really only just at the beginning.

RUTH: But how long is it going to take?

DAVID: Probably as long as we're here.

RUTH: And you really don't mind all the disruption?

ANNE: Oh, now and then I get disheartened and wish we'd never started. But it doesn't last long. It's so lovely to see what's emerging.

RUTH: But what about the cost? All that labour must be costing you a fortune!

DAVID: No. That's the best thing about it. We couldn't quite believe it either when we were told. You see, it isn't costing us a penny. The whole thing has already been paid for.

ANNE: By the Landlord.

*Barbara Sumner*

# 32 The Right Credentials

THEME

Ephesians 2:8–9.

CAST

CUSTOMS OFFICER (CO).
ASSISTANT.
MAN and WOMAN.

COSTUME AND PROPS

A table and two chairs. Various papers and an envelope. All characters should be dressed conventionally.

SCRIPT

| | |
|---|---|
| CO: | [*To WOMAN, handing back papers.*] Thank you madam. If you'll just follow that gentleman he'll lead you through. |
| WOMAN: | [*Obviously happy.*] Many thanks. |
| ASSISTANT: | [*To WOMAN.*] Welcome home! We've been expecting you. |
| WOMAN: | Yes, I've been looking forward to this so much. [*Walks off talking to ASSISTANT.*] |
| MAN: | [*To CO.*] I'm sure I've seen that lady before somewhere. Let me think.... |
| CO: | Excuse me sir, can I have a look at your papers please? |
| MAN: | Papers? Oh, you mean these things from my interview. [*Pointing to interview room.*] That chap certainly asked some funny questions! [*Hands over the envelope, then begins to reminisce while CO looks through documents.*] I'm quite looking forward to some peace and quiet. I've had a pretty hectic life. |
| CO: | Yes, I can see. |
| MAN: | Mind you, I did enjoy it. Bit of a whiz-kid really: |

jet setter in my youth, a top executive, JP, Church Warden, Chairman of many charities. All hard work, but then I've always been a hard worker. Yes, I'm really looking forward to some peace and quiet. [*Sudden change of face.*] I say, it won't be too quiet will it? I mean, we won't be sitting round all day doing nothing will we? I've never fancied the idea of all those harps and angelic...

CO: [*Interrupts.*] I'm sorry sir, but I'm afraid you're not being admitted.

MAN: [*Bewildered.*] What? Well there must be some kind of mistake.

CO: No mistake sir, you haven't got the right credentials.

MAN: But surely you must have overlooked something. [*Becoming angry.*] I've worked hard to get here you know. I've abided by all the rules and regulations. There are no black stains on my character. You can't classify me as an undesireable alien.

CO: Your credentials show clearly that you are not of this kingdom sir, this must have become clear in your interview.

MAN: He talked about passports and sponsors and motives and lots of other irrelevant things. But you all know I've been a JP *and* a Church Warden. I've been a real contributor. [*Becoming desperate.*] My boss has written an excellent reference. I'm a man of very high character—of very high standards.

CO: It all depends on what standards you set sir. I'm afraid that for entry you require the highest standards: perfection.

MAN: Well that's impossible—nobody's perfect.

CO: Quite right sir.

MAN: Well then nobody should get in.

CO: Right again sir, nobody *should* get in.

MAN: But that woman got in—and I remember now—yes she appeared before in a court on several occasions and was found guilty. Look what *is* going on?

CO: The lady gained entry because she had the right credentials—her sponsor covered for her. So although she hadn't reached the required standard on her own, she got in on his passport.

MAN: Well who is this sponsor and why haven't I heard of him?

CO: Oh but you have sir, you have.

MAN: Look aren't we simply talking at cross purposes?

CO: Cross purposes—yes sir, I think that's really what it's all about.

*Len Browne*

# 33 The Salt of the Earth

## THEME

Matthew 5:13.

## CAST

Miss Lottie CRUET, a shop assistant.
A smart polite MAN.

## COSTUME AND PROPS

Modern dress and minimum props to suggest a small hardware store.

## SCRIPT

Miss CRUET is busying herself behind counter when MAN enters.

MAN: Morning.
CRUET: Good morning.
MAN: Look, I'm really sorry to be a pain, but I'm afraid I've got a complaint about a salt pot I bought yesterday.
CRUET: I see. What seems to be the problem?
MAN: Well, I was in a bit of a hurry so I didn't look very closely, and when I got it home I realised it didn't have a hole in the top.
CRUET: No, that's right; it wouldn't have.
MAN: I beg your pardon.
CRUET: It wouldn't have, that's the new line.
MAN: Well look. I'm sorry if I appear a little slow, but if there's no hole in the top, how do I get the salt out of the pot?
CRUET: You don't. That's the point. Isn't it good?
MAN: *What's* the point? I don't think it's good at all, I think it's just silly.
CRUET: Look. It hasn't got a hole in the top—to protect the salt.

MAN: From what?

CRUET: Well if you really want to know—from the cruel world outside. As if salt hasn't gone through enough already. There it has lain for hundreds of years in some wonderful corner of the world like Siberia. It gets hacked about with some miner's axe, and then ground into tiny pieces in some lame excuse for a concentration camp known as a mill. And then when it at last reaches the haven of your salt pot, well all you can think about is putting it through the same grisly nightmare again. Well I say, have a heart.

MAN: I don't think we're on the same wavelength at all are we?

CRUET: Why not? Don't you understand?

MAN: Well I must confess I'm having some difficulty. What's all this 'grisly nightmare' business. Mine's a very nice home.

CRUET: 'What's all this grisly nightmare business'? As if you can't guess.

MAN: I can't.

CRUET: Well I'll tell you then. It's being tipped out of a pot to fall maybe hundreds of millimetres to your plate. It's landing on roasting hot beef and Yorkshire. It's seeing the steely blade of your knife bearing down upon it. It's seeing your gleaming well-toothed mouth opening wide and slavering. It's being chewed to bits in your champing chops. It's crawling like a slave down your all-conquering gullet. That's the 'grisly nightmare'. It's a very dangerous world outside of that salt pot.

MAN: Yes, I think I'm coming to see your point. So, what do you have in mind?

CRUET: I have in mind a world of holeless salt pots. Communities where salt at last can be free to live in peace, without fear, where grain shall live with grain in true brotherhood, accepted and loved. Released from the terror of this cruel world.

MAN: But...but my salt actually likes salting my food.

CRUET: Oh yes, we've all heard that one before.

MAN: It does. That's why it exists—to salt things and bring new flavour and excitement to eating.

CRUET: It all sounds a bit selfish to me.

MAN: How?

CRUET: Well it sounds as though the salt has really got the good end of the deal doesn't it? As long as it's at your service, seeking to make your life a better place, you're quite happy. Try and protect the stuff and you get all uppitty. Look sir. Take this salt pot. Be a pioneer. Let your salt mind it's own business while you mind yours, mmmm?

MAN: Well if you put it like that, I suppose I have been a bit selfish in the past. But I'm very sorry. Yes, you're right. I'll take this one home and do my bit. I'll do my bit to make the world a better place for salt.
Goodbye and thank you Miss...?

CRUET: Cruet, but you can call me Lottie.

*Tim Mayfield*

# 34 John

## THEME

The folly of people hardening their hearts against God.

## CAST

The script can be read or recited by one person. Alternatively several people can be involved taking the parts of John, parents, teachers, boss, doctor, God the Father and Jesus.

## COSTUME AND PROPS

Jeans and T-shirts or conventional dress and equipment, eg, teacher holding books, etc.
The part of God the Father could be read via a microphone and loudspeaker, so that he is not seen.

## SCRIPT

He was a boy much like any other; we shall call him, for the sake of parable, John.

When he was a child, his parents said to him, 'We are only substitute parents. Your true father, whom you have never loved, can really look after you, protecting you from everything, from bad driving to black magic. He lives in the Mansion House, where you cannot go yet, but he is waiting for you at King's Cross, and he will give you the ticket.'

But John did not listen, as he preferred his box of chocolates. So he went back and played in the pig-sty.

The years passed and he went to school, where his teachers said to him, 'We are only substitute teachers. Your true instructor, whom you have never heard, wants to show you the secret of life; he knows you better than any Aptitude Tests or Marriage Guidance Council. He lives in the Mansion House, where you cannot go yet, but he is waiting for you at King's Cross, and he will give you the ticket.'

But John thought, 'What a drag!' So he went back and scribbled in the pig-sty.

The years passed and he got a job, but his boss said to him, 'I'm only a substitute boss. Your true employer, whom you have never served, doesn't pay by the hour, but hands over his entire fortune, the most glittering treasure in the universe. He lives in the Mansion House, where you cannot go yet, but he is waiting for you at King's Cross, and he will give you the ticket.'

But John muttered, 'I've got my pride, you know; I want to earn my own living.' So he went back and scrapped around from nine till five in the pig-sty.

The years passed and he had to retire because of ill-health. The doctor said to him, 'I'm only a substitute doctor. Your true physician, whom you have never consulted, isn't foxed by old age and death; he can give you a life-transplant and cut out the sin-cancer. He lives in the Mansion House, but he is waiting for you at King's Cross and he will give you the ticket.'

But John sighed, 'Don't go on at me, I've heard it all before. There's nothing wrong with me; I've always done my best—nearly. And anyway, I don't believe this Mansion House place exists; you're just saying it to frighten me.' So he went back and wallowed in the pig-sty.

The years passed and he died; and in the Mansion House, as the sumptuous banquet began, his place was empty. God said, 'Where's John?' With a tear in his eye, the King said, 'He never came to my Cross. He chose the pig-sty.' 'How sad,' said God, 'how tragically sad.'

*Lance Pierson*

# 35 Numbers

THEME

The logic of belief in God.

CAST

ROB, a mathematics lecturer. ANDY, a member of the audience or congregation, who should be sitting in the front with it.

SCRIPT

ROB comes through the audience/congregation from the back.

ROB: Wow! There must be 300 people in this room: that's 600 legs and 3,000 toes, working on the national average, probably around 34.3 verrucas and about 6,240 teeth, and looking at you lot, about 4,830 fillings. Don't you just love numbers? I do. Numbers make my life worth living. They give me a reason to get up in the morning. 'Course I haven't always been able to count, but now I can count anywhere I like. Some people worship God, but me, I worship numbers. They're infinite, they surround us, their complexity goes beyond the limits of our minds, and yet they're so simple—[*to ANDY in front*] like you are!

Hey, you've seen Christians trying to get people to come to church, but me, I'm trying to drag people to a maths lecture. Some people call me a numbers freak or a binary basher. But who cares? We've all got to stand up and be counted one day.

Hey you! Come here. Do you want to come to a maths lecture?

ANDY: No thanks, mate.
ROB: Why?
ANDY: I'm busy.
ROB: But it'll be brilliant.
ANDY: I'm not clever enough.
ROB: But maths is for all levels. What is two plus two?

ANDY: Four.
ROB: There you go.
ANDY: Look, I just don't want to go.
ROB: There's going to be coffee after.
ANDY: Great. Sit through a boring maths lecture for a grotty cup of coffee...out of plastic cups I bet, as well.
ROB: We've got biscuits too.
ANDY: Give me a break.
ROB: Kit Kats? [*ANDY gives ROB a piercing look.*] Nothing?
ANDY: Anyway, I don't believe in it.
ROB: In what?
ANDY: I don't believe in numbers.
ROB: What do you mean, you don't believe in numbers. Our world couldn't exist without numbers, they're everywhere, everything revolves around numbers.
ANDY: I don't believe in them.
ROB: But believing in numbers is the most logical thing in the world.
ANDY: Well if they're so logical, tell me this. Is the number three a number all by itself, or is it made up of three individual number ones.
ROB: It's both. It's a three, and it's three ones.
ANDY: I can't believe that, it's either one or the other.
ROB: But $1 + 1 + 1 = 3$ is a basic assumption in maths.
ANDY: Assumption!
ROB: But even the most famous mathematician there's ever been assumed that.
ANDY: And who's that then?
ROB: Pythagorus.
ANDY: And who's Pythagorus?
ROB: He's an historical figure.
ANDY: Oh, so now you're expecting me to believe myths and legends handed down from generation to generation.
ROB: No, there's documented evidence.
ANDY: You only believe in numbers because you've been indoctrinated.
ROB: What?
ANDY: I bet you were brought up in a home where your mum and dad believed in numbers.
ROB: Yes...

ANDY: And you went to a school where they taught compulsory maths.

ROB: Of course.

ANDY: Add to that the propaganda from the media...you've been indoctrinated.

ROB: But everyone uses numbers.

ANDY: That's my very point. Everyone except me. I've broken free. I don't use numbers anymore. I use letters. My telephone code is EAGGHG. To phone the police I dial III. I watch BBC A, BBC B, ITV and Channel D, and the time now, according to my analogue watch, is J past F.

ROB: [*Calmly.*] All right then, what about money?

ANDY: American Express?

ROB: That's different.

ANDY: Thank you.

ROB: But don't you see, that just because you don't believe in numbers doesn't mean they don't exist. Just because you don't think something's relevant, doesn't mean it isn't relevant.

ANDY: But I'm sincere, what more d'you want?

ROB: But you could be sincerely wrong. If the truth is, let's assume for a moment, that numbers do exist, then it doesn't make an ounce of difference that you say they don't exist.

ANDY: Come on. Next you'll be expecting me to believe God exists!

ROB: There are some things in life that exist whether people choose to ignore them or not. Otherwise life just doesn't add up.

*Trapdoor Theatre Company*

# 36 Lead Us Not Into...

THEME

Temptation. This is something with which we all battle, and the devil's whispering words can be as real as portrayed here. (Mt 6:13, or Lk 11:4.)

CAST

JENNY.
DEVIL.

COSTUME

JENNY—very ordinarily dressed, thus representing anyone in the congregation.
DEVIL—should be clearly identified, but not made to look ridiculous. Some make-up may help.

SCRIPT

[*JENNY is sitting at a table, reading. On the table is a large cream-cake. She looks up from the book.*]

JENNY: Hmm, that looks rather tasty...good job I'm on a diet...otherwise I'd be temped to...er...no.
[*She continues reading.*]

DEVIL: Since when? What about all that food you put away at lunch time?

JENNY: Mind you, when I think of all that food I put away at lunch time....

DEVIL: What difference will that make?

JENNY: What difference will that make?

DEVIL: Exactly.
[*She goes on reading.*]

JENNY: No. It's probably synthetic cream anyway.

DEVIL: [*Casually.*] It's not ya know.
[*She leans forward, taking a close look.*]

JENNY: It's not ya know. Ooh, and there's a huge dollop of

cream that's about to fall off the plate. I wouldn't want it to mark the table.

DEVIL: Quite right.

JENNY: But all that sugar....

DEVIL: Sugar's good for you. And just look at that jam.

JENNY: Ooh, I didn't notice that jam before. I wonder if it's...

[*She dips a finger in and tastes it.*]

DEVIL: }
JENNY: } Yes, it's strawberry!

DEVIL: Oh, look out the cream's going. Oh well caught.

[*JENNY swallows a finger full.*]

JENNY: Mmmm...but what about the diet?

DEVIL: Well, you've ruined it for today, now. Tell you what, I've got a good idea—

JENNY: I'll start tomorrow!

DEVIL: Exactly.

JENNY: Mmmmmm...nice...

DEVIL: But naughty.

[*Both freeze.*]

*Dave Hopwood*

# 37 Alter Ego

THEME

Problems in prayer.

CAST

ADRIAN.
VOICE, which should be amplified over a sound-system and not unamplified from the wings.

COSTUME AND PROPS

A chair centre-stage and a small table to one side with a Bible and notebook on it.

SCRIPT

[*ADRIAN enters and mimes cleaning his teeth and washing his face. He moves to chair and removes slippers. He mimes turning bed-covers back. He opens the Bible, leaving it on the table, and mimes kneeling at bedside as though in prayer. He turns to pick up notebook and holds it in front of him.*]

ADRIAN: Oh Lord, I do thank you that you are a great God and worthy of all praise. Thank you that I am redeemed, that you are my Saviour...
VOICE: Adrian?
ADRIAN: Thank you for the forgiveness of sins...
VOICE: Adrian!
ADRIAN: Lord, you know that I want to be the best for you, the best I can possibly be.
VOICE: Adrian, just say what's on your heart...
ADRIAN: I feel like I've let you down a bit today, I'm sorry.
VOICE: I forgive you. Tell me about it.
ADRIAN: But thank you that I know I have the victory in you.
VOICE: Adrian, you're doing it again.
ADRIAN: Please help me to hold on to that truth much more. [*Moves to open Bible.*]
VOICE: [*Sharply.*] No, don't go and change the subject, Adrian.

ADRIAN: Lord, I thank you for your word. [*Looks at Bible passage.*] 2 Corinthians 12 really spoke to me today, especially that bit about boasting—that really spoke to me.

VOICE: Did it?

ADRIAN: And about being weak.

VOICE: Ah!

ADRIAN: Thank you for the word which says 'when we are weak we are strong'.

VOICE: Oh, that's all right, but...

ADRIAN: And please help me to be more patient.

VOICE: Wait a minute I...

ADRIAN: Especially with my family.

VOICE: Hey, slow down!

ADRIAN: I really try with them Lord; but honestly, sometimes they're enough to make a saint swear—if you get my meaning.

VOICE: [*As though to someone else next to him.*] What is this? A prayer or a shopping list?

ADRIAN: Please, please help me to be more patient with them.

VOICE: Of course I will—if you'll let me! Suppose you tell me what happened today?

ADRIAN: And please bless Mark with his exams.

VOICE: There you go again!

ADRIAN: Help him to do really well.

VOICE: Why do you keep changing the subject?

ADRIAN: Mind you, he's so brainy he doesn't need me to pray for him—I ought to be praying for the examiners!

VOICE: That's the problem isn't it, Adrian? You resent Mark doing better than you did.

ADRIAN: Lord, thank you that Mark finds exams so much easier than I ever did, I'm so pleased...

VOICE: Liar!

ADRIAN: Please help me to be a good brother to him. [*Stops, having come as close to the real problem as he will allow himself to come.*]

VOICE: Adrian, when will you stop pretending? Be honest with me please, I can't help you unless you are.

*Max Carpenter*

# 38 Bodywork

## THEME

The church, the body of Christ. (1 Corinthians 12.)

## CAST

EARS, EYES, BRAIN, MOUTH, HANDS, FEET, and NOSE.
POLICEMAN.

## COSTUMES

The parts of the body dressed in jeans and T-shirt with names or pictures round each neck. The local police may be prepared to lend a uniform. (This is best performed as a radio sketch without visible cast.)

## SCRIPT

Before the sketch begins it should be explained that the scene is inside a car.

EYES: Cor! Isn't it a glorious day for a drive in the country, Ears?

EARS: Isn't it just, Eyes. Can you hear that lovely birdsong?
[*SFX: sounds of spring.*]

EYES: Well of course I can't, Ears, but I can see this lovely scenery. Look at that little wood down there!

NOSE: I bet none of you can smell that horrible manure.

EARS: Oh shut up, Nose!

NOSE: Phyor! That's disgusting!

EARS: Typical. You always ruin it!

EYES: Yeah, blinkin' Nose—always sticking it in.

NOSE: Well it's all right for you, you can't smell it. Cor! Wind the window up a bit, hands.

HANDS: Hang on a sec, I've got a gear change coming up.

FEET: Can I have a bit of peace and quiet up there! I've got the brakes and the gears to work!

EYES: Watch out, Brain!

BRAIN: What!

EYES: That car's pulled out on you!
[*SFX: screech of brakes.*]

BRAIN: Give him what for, Hands!
[*SFX: angry car horn.*]

BRAIN: And mouth!

MOUTH: You stupid idiot!

BRAIN: Thank you, gentlemen.

FEET: As usual, no one thinks of me. I slam the brakes on, don't I? But no one thinks of me. It's awful, being a foot. Shut away all day down here in the dark with smelly horrible socks. I've always wanted to be a... a mouth!

MOUTH: Well it's not that easy, you know.

FEET: Really?

MOUTH: It isn't! You've got all that bad breath to put up with as well as regular brushing with a recommended stripey blinkin' toothpaste.

BRAIN: It's for your own good, Mouth. I've told you before.

MOUTH: And you can belt up, Brain, for a start. Without us, what would you be? A lump of grey jelly on a driving seat.

EYES: Yeah, you wouldn't even be able to see without me.

EARS: Or hear.

EYES: Well, he could get by without hearing, well enough.

HANDS: OK, then! Let's try driving *without* the hands for a bit.

FEET: What?

BRAIN: Come off it, old chap!

HANDS: Yeah! Then we'll soon see about that. Try driving without *me* for a bit.

BRAIN: No! Eyes!

EYES: No! Let's teach those upstart little hands a lesson or two.

BRAIN: Eyes! Open up! Quick!

[*SFX: an almighty car crash. Pause. Sound of police siren getting nearer. Screech of brakes. Slam of door.*]

POLICEMAN: Good afternoon, sir. Just blow into this little bag please.

NOSE: Hmph! I thought I could smell trouble brewing.

CHORUS: Oh shut up, Nose!

POLICEMAN: Who said that, sir?

*Peter Chantry*

# 39 The Cake

## THEME

The church, the body of Christ. (1 Corinthians 12.)

## CAST AND COSTUME

NARRATOR—a recipe book with the script in.
FLOUR—mattress cover or blue sleeping-bag with a white panel saying McDougalls.
STORK—margarine tub lid hung round neck.
SUGAR—might carry a silver spoon; pink-and-white clothing.
SALT—a Saxa symbol. Or dress in white.
COCOA—punk, tramp, ethnic dress depending on character chosen.
EGG—a cardboard egg with a lion stamped on the front. Dress in white and yellow.
CREAM—quite smart cream-coloured clothes.

## SCRIPT

[*To be performed in a bold, pantomime-type style, with lots of energy. As the characters enter they form a horse-shoe beside the narrator.*]

NARRATOR: Good morning and welcome to today's cookery demonstration. We're starting with something jolly simple and really quite fool-proof—the sponge cake. So without further ado. First take six ounces of flour.
[*Enter FLOUR holding a flower.*]

NARRATOR: No, I'm sorry. I meant *flour.*
[*FLOUR looks offended and exits. Re-enters dressed as FLOUR.*]

FLOUR: Here, I am all raring to go. [*To audience.*] I'm always the first ingredient. It's because I'm the most important. I'm the biggest too.

NARRATOR: Sieve the flour into the mixing-bowl.

FLOUR: Hey, hang on a minute! I'm not too keen on this being sieved bit. I trust that you're not implying

| | |
|---|---|
| | I'm lumpy or anything. There's nothing wrong with me you know. I'm quite all right as I am. I will *not* be sieved. |
| NARRATOR: | Weigh out a similar quantity of butter. Do we have any butter? [*A voice off stage says, 'Go on'.*] [*Enter STORK margarine on one leg.*] |
| STORK: | Please sir, I'm not butter, I'm only margarine. |
| NARRATOR: | Why are you standing on one leg? |
| STORK: | I'm Stork margarine of course. But I'll be hopping along now. I'm not really what you want, I'm not really good enough. You really want butter. |
| NARRATOR: | No, no, please stay. We do need you, any fat will do. |
| STORK: | [*Offended.*] I'm not fat—I only weigh six ounces. |
| NARRATOR: | That's great, you're exactly what we need. |
| STORK: | Well I'm not sure, but if you think I'll do. |
| NARRATOR: | Mix in six ounces of sugar. [*Enter SUGAR very effeminate and extremely vain.*] |
| SUGAR: | Who wants me? I heard someone call my name. [*To audience.*] I'm incredibly popular you know, in fact I have people eating out of my bag. Well, what did you want? |
| NARRATOR: | Mix six ounces of sugar with the flour and margarine. |
| SUGAR: | Well I'm quite happy as I am thank you, I certainly don't want to mix with the likes of them—flour and margarine, not even butter. |
| STORK: | There you are I told you so. I'm not wanted. |
| NARRATOR: | Now just hang on a minute. We're trying to make a cake and we need sugar. |
| SUGAR: | Well I think that's a super idea, but I'm quite happy thanks, people seem to like me just as I am. I'm OK on my own. |
| NARRATOR: | Add a pinch of salt. [*Enter SALT.*] |
| SALT: | What's all this about a pinch? You wanted six ounces of them? There's plenty of me and I want to be fully involved. |
| NARRATOR: | But you'll totally dominate the flavour. You |

won't be able to taste any of the other ingredients. It wouldn't be a cake at all.

SALT: Oh come on, change the recipe. They don't seem too keen anyway, and here I am as keen as anything. Forget about them, use more of me.

NARRATOR: It wouldn't work. We need them and we need you, but in the right proportions. Add cocoa powder to taste.

[*Enter COCOA, blacked up. COCOA represents 'The Outsider' and so can be adapted to whatever character will fit most accurately into that category for your audience, eg, punk, tramp, black person, woman(!) COCOA's script will obviously need adapting.*]

ALL: Well we're certainly not going to mix with *him.*

SUGAR: [*Stepping forward.*] 'Add to taste'—he's not to our taste at all. You can't expect us to mix with him, he might contaminate us.

NARRATOR: That's the whole idea, it's a chocolate cake and he flavours you all. You complement one another, you're designed to go together. [*They shake heads.*] Oh well. Break in three eggs.

[*Enter EGG.*]

EGG: Phew! It's boiling in here. Just my little yoke—get it? What do I do?

NARRATOR: Break three eggs into the bowl.

EGG: You mean damage my beautiful shell? No way! That would be far too painful. You must think I'm cracking up if you expect me to open myself up—and in front of all these ingredients. No, I couldn't do it, it would be far too painful.

NARRATOR: But that's what you're designed for—you are far more valuable when you're broken.

Finally spread cream between the two layers of sponge.

[*Enter CREAM.*]

CREAM: I'd rather go on top, I'm sure I'd be better appreciated there. I feel I'd be rather wasted in the middle. I'm the most important you know, after all, I'm the most expensive ingredient.

FLOUR: You're not the most important. I am—I'm by far the biggest.

SUGAR: I'm the nicest, though. I can't imagine anyone eating flour straight out of the bag, nor for that matter margarine.

STORK: You see I'm right, no one wants me. I'm not good enough for this cake.

COCOA: Hey man, don't despair! You're not the only one who's not appreciated around here. Some ingredients get above themselves.

FLOUR: Who's getting above themselves?

[*The scene degenerates into everyone arguing with their neighbour in pairs.*]

COCOA: Cool it! This is stupid. We aren't getting anywhere standing around here arguing. I'm not so perfect I wouldn't mind changing a bit. I'm going to risk it, I'm getting into the bowl.

[*He jumps into the bowl and starts rotating. The others watch and then one by one they follow suit. They go round and round and then bind together arms around each other's shoulders and freeze.*]

NARRATOR: Mr God makes exceedingly good cakes.

*Lucy Willis*

# 40 Angels

THEME

Christian witness.

CAST

ANGEL.
SUSAN BUTLER (or another first name can be chosen).
GOD (via an amplified voice off stage).

COSTUME AND PROPS

The ANGEL should wear traditional long white dress or alb with wings and halo. Underneath this there should be T-shirt and jeans. SUSAN BUTLER in everyday clothes.

SCRIPT

[*'Hallelujah chorus' on tape. Or other music, if preferred. Enter traditional-looking ANGEL.*]

| | |
|---|---|
| ANGEL: | Lord? I say, Lord? How do I look? You said I was to be an angel, if you remember? I think I've got the costume right. This is the sort of thing they all wear in paintings and stained-glass windows, so I thought. |
| GOD: | Take it all off. |
| ANGEL: | Sorry? |
| GOD: | Take it all off. |
| ANGEL: | Take all what off, Lord? |
| GOD: | That ridiculous tat. |
| ANGEL: | I say, Lord, that's a bit steep, dash it. |
| GOD: | All of it. |
| ANGEL: | What a swiz! |
| GOD: | Now! |
| ANGEL: | But I looked at this absolutely super book with the most marvellous angel cozies in it. |
| GOD: | Off! |

ANGEL: Jolly unfair I call it. I bet Gabriel didn't get this sort of treatment.

GOD: Butler! Butler!

[*Enter SUSAN BUTLER.*]

SUSAN BUTLER: Yeah?

GOD: Remove those ridiculous clothes.

SUSAN BUTLER: All right. [*Starts to remove her clothes.*]

GOD: No, not yours. There's Christians out there. His.

SUSAN BUTLER: Oh right.

ANGEL: I say, Lord, you don't actually have a Butler, do you?

GOD: She's on an MSC scheme.

ANGEL: Gosh, do you have an MSC scheme in heaven?

GOD: Sometimes even we have to doctor the unemployment figures.

SUSAN BUTLER: And he only got me because he asked for a Butler, and my name's Butler. Susan Butler.

ANGEL: Yes, but gosh, I mean, a Butler?

SUSAN BUTLER: All right, so he's still an elitist. But at least he's appointed a woman butler. He's not sexist anymore.

GOD: One step at a time.

ANGEL: Surely I don't have to take off the wings?

GOD: Especially the wings.

ANGEL: But no one will accept me as your angel dressed like this. [*Takes off alb and wings and is dressed in T-shirt and jeans.*] I just look dead ordinary.

GOD: It's dead ordinary people that I call.

ANGEL: But in all the pictures and windows they're not ordinary people, they're all wearing these amazing clothes and shining all superly bright, and...

GOD: Oh don't be so childish. Can't you see they're just pictures?

SUSAN BUTLER: Listen, creep—what is your name, anyway?

ANGEL: Well, it's Nigel, actually.

SUSAN BUTLER: If I may take the liberty of pointing it out to you, Nigel, the word 'angel' simply means 'messenger'. And the Lord calls ordinary people to be his messengers, which is pretty cool of him really, when you think of the sort of wallies who get sent. I mean, fancy you being sent.

ANGEL: I think you're a real spoil-sport, Lord. When you said I was to be an angel, I thought you meant something dramatic, and exciting, like. POW!—and everyone would know I had come from you as your special messenger.

[*Exclamation of wrath from God.*]

ANGEL: What's he saying?

SUSAN BUTLER: He's narked because you're another of the 'I want flashing lights in heaven' brigade.

ANGEL: You mean there aren't going to be flashing lights either? Are we having to make cuts like everyone else?

GOD: Ever heard of faith? You'll have to learn that I don't go in for special effects.

ANGEL: Well how will people know, if they don't see any special effects, that I'm your messenger?

SUSAN BUTLER: You must go...

ANGEL: Dressed like this?

SUSAN BUTLER: Dressed like that. To speak the truth as you see it.

ANGEL: Can't I at least have a halo?

GOD: No.

ANGEL: Just a small one?

GOD: No. Speak the truth as best you can. And people will decide for themselves what to make of you.

ANGEL: They may decide wrongly. They may not recognise me as your messenger. They may not give me the proper respect.

SUSAN BUTLER: It wouldn't be the first time that's happened. So won't it be exciting, not knowing how they'll treat you?

ANGEL: I might fail. I might get hurt.
SUSAN BUTLER: You might.
ANGEL: I think I'd rather not go.
SUSAN BUTLER: Tough.
GOD: I've called you to go, so go.
ANGEL: Well just play me out with the music will you?
GOD: [*When music begins—'Hallelujah chorus' again.*] Now go. [*Exit ANGEL.*] Butler!
SUSAN BUTLER: Yeah?
GOD: Go and burn the tat.
SUSAN BUTLER: Right.
GOD: If he's a good witness the wings he needs will grow.
[*'Hallelujah Chorus', briefly. Exit SUSAN BUTLER.*]

*Jabbok Theatre*

# 41 'Love is...'

THEME

To show that loving God gives us responsibilities to the world.

CAST

Six or eight people in a chorus line facing the congregation.
Two narrators (N1 and N2), one either side of the chorus line.

COSTUME

Jeans and T-shirts.

SCRIPT

[*Each piece of action for the chorus line is a freeze frame. Each line should take its time, so the sketch should not be rushed.*]

N1: Love God. [*The whole chorus line clasp their hands in prayer.*]

N2: Hate your enemies. [*They throttle one another.*]

N1: Love God. [*Clasp their hands always on this line.*]

N2: Ignore other people. [*Folded arms they turn their backs on each other.*]

N1: Love God.

N2: Despise your friends. [*They turn and shake hands sneeringly.*]

N1: Love God.

N2: Ignore wallies. [*The chorus turns and ignores the person at the end of the chorus line.*]

N1: Love God.

N2: Hate bullies. [*Fighting position.*]

N1: Love the world. [*Each person in chorus assumes sinful position.*]

N2: Ignore God. [*Middle person in chorus becomes a crucifix, all the others cower away.*]
[*Lengthy pause.*]

N1: Love God. [*Chorus line open hands in prayer—change in attitude.*]

N2: Love your enemies. [*People on the end fold arms, those on the inside of them place their hand on the enemy's shoulder.*]

N2: Love God.

N1: Pray for those who persecute you. [*Half the chorus remain prayerful, the other half act as if to hit their neighbour.*]

N2: Love God.

N1: Love your friends. [*Appropriate handshakes, hugs, etc.*]

N2: Love God.

N1: Love your neighbour. [*Whole chorus line with arms outstretched to audience.*]

N2: [*Chorus return to line.*] And the man asked Jesus 'Who is my neighbour?'

N1: }<br>N2: } Love people...

CHORUS: ...because God loves *you*! [*Points to audience.*]

*Si Jones*

# 42 Hare-sterical

## THEME

Worry. Based directly on Matthew 6:25–34, which is read during the sketch, possibly by a child who can be heard well.

## CAST AND COSTUME

WHITE RABBIT (from *Alice in Wonderland*)—dressed in white with yellow waistcoat and big ears. Should jump about, flinging hands in the air and racing around without ever really staying still. Has a high-pitched, excited voice.
BROWN RABBIT (from Cadbury's Caramel advert)—dressed in brown with red scarf and big ears. Should be laid back, hardly moving throughout. Voice like melting butter.

## SKETCH

[*Enter BROWN RABBIT, calmly. He settles himself, leaning or reclining on something. Suddenly WHITE RABBIT enters behind audience, running around, jumping up and down in a panic. Finally he makes it to the front, repeatedly saying:*]

WHITE RABBIT: Oh dear, oh dear, oh dear!

BROWN RABBIT: What's up, Doc?

WHITE RABBIT: What's up? What's up he says. [*Pacing across stage.*] Everything's up. I've got food to get, clothes to buy, money to make, a life to build. Oh dear, oh dear, oh dear! Oh dear, oh dear, oh dear!

BROWN RABBIT: Hang on, aren't you forgetting something?

WHITE RABBIT: Oh no, I haven't forgotten something have I? Oh dear, oh dear, oh dear! Now I'll never get anywhere. [*Starts pulling hair out.*] Oh dear, oh dear, oh dear!

BROWN RABBIT: Whoa, slow down a second. [*Stopping him as he goes past.*] Why all the panic?

WHITE RABBIT: Because there's so much to worry about. [*Fidgeting on the spot.*]

BROWN RABBIT: But you're forgetting what Jesus said.

WHITE RABBIT: [*Stops fidgeting.*] What Jesus said?

BROWN RABBIT: Yes, he told his followers not to get all panicky over food and clothes and things.

WHITE RABBIT: He did? Where? [*Very interested.*]

BROWN RABBIT: Right here, halfway through Matthew chapter 6, verses 25 to 34.

[*At this point the reading should begin while the two rabbits pretend to read their own Bible.*]

WHITE RABBIT: Wow! Did he say that? [*Very excited.*]

BROWN RABBIT: It's down here in black and white.

WHITE RABBIT: That's terrific, now I don't have to worry! Hooray! [*Jumps for joy.*] That makes me feel a whole lot better. [*Skips around BROWN RABBIT.*] Now I don't have to care about anything.

BROWN RABBIT: Hey, he never said that. There's a big difference between not worrying and not caring.

WHITE RABBIT: Oh, so take care but don't worry, right?

BROWN RABBIT: Right. Fancy a choccy bar?

*Stairs and Whispers Theatre Company*

# 43 A Little Bit of Soap

## THEME

To highlight the danger of the church becoming preoccupied with its own maintenance and forgetting the needs of the world outside.

## CAST

Three people.

## COSTUME AND PROPS

Towels, bowls, flannels, etc. These props may be mimed. Costume is unimportant.

## SCRIPT

[*Enter 1, 2 and 3 carrying bowls, towels and flannels. They place the bowls down and begin washing meticulously. 1 sighs heavily. 2 and 3 look at him, then continue. 1 sighs heavily again. Then does so a third time.*]

2: What's wrong now?
1: I don't think I'll ever get this stain off.
2: Yes you will, just keep washing.
1: But I just keep getting dirty again.
3: I agree. I've messed up these hands so many times you wouldn't believe it.
2: As long as we keep washing they'll come clean eventually. [*To 1.*] Oh, you missed a bit there.
1: Just think—it'll be great when we're all clean. No more dirt—no more problems. [*Looks at 2.*] Look at the state of your thumb!
2: Yours isn't much better.
1: You shouldn't be looking at my dirt.
2: You started it!
3: Er, has anyone got any baby powder?
2: [*Ignoring this.*] How are your nails these days?
[*3 holds them up.*]

2: Hmm, I should forget the baby powder and try sheep dip if I were you.

3: I have! You told me to before.

2: I feel sorry for the sheep, then!

1: Hello! [*Looks off stage.*] I think there's someone at the door.

2: Don't be distracted, brother, keep washing.

3: But one of us had better see who it is [*turns to 1*], hadn't you?

1: But I'm nearly clean now, if I touch that door handle.... Oh, all right. [*Exits.*]

2: Hey! Look at that! [*Holds up left hand.*] I've actually done my middle finger, I'd forgotten what it looked like.

1: [*Re-entering.*] It's, er, some tramp chappie—he wants some money.

2: Do you know, money is one of the biggest germ carriers around? A £5 note under a microscope is obscene!

3: Well, a 50p can't be too bad, give him that.

1: I am not putting my hands in these pockets—you don't know what's been in them.

2: Didn't you tell him we're busy getting clean?

1: He didn't seem to understand that. What can we do?

2: I know. There's a spare bowl over there. If he comes in, we'll give him that. What are his hands like?

1: The colour of the M1!

2: Ugh!

3: But that's a good idea. He'll like a good wash. Just what he needs. Tell him there's a spare bowl in here. Go on.

[*1 exits again, muttering.*]

2: I've had this idea of a midweek washing session—you know, meeting in people's homes on a Wednesday, then we can wash our hands during the week as well. What d'you think?

3: It'll never work. *Sportsnight* is on a Wednesday.

1: [*Re-enters.*] That's strange.

3: Didn't he want the bowl?

1: He'd gone.

2: Typical. And we could have helped him get clean. [*Stops and looks at 1.*] You didn't touch him, did you?

1: No. But I put my hands in my pockets.
2 and 3: Ugh! [*2 throws him a flannel.*] Get washing!
[*All freeze.*]

*Dave Hopwood*

# 44 Green Piece

THEME

Ecology.

CAST

An ordinary MAN, kneeling at prayer in his bedroom.
ANGEL—it does not matter if the congregation never realise who the angel is—he merely represents the voice of God.

COSTUME AND PROPS

Both could be in jeans and T-shirt, or the MAN could be in pyjamas, dressing-gown and slippers.

As much or as little props as is felt appropriate. Kneeling at a bedside could be mimed.

SCRIPT

MAN: Lord, I pray for my family. Bless them this night and keep them safe. Especially watch over Calvin in Ireland tonight, please bring him back safely to us. And Lord, I do pray also for our church, after that sermon this week on the world's needs. Lord, please could you watch over the world's resources; and all this controversy with the ozone layer—could you please cover that up; the hole I mean, not the controversy! Lord, save us from ourselves. We seem so intent on destroying our own resources. Lord, protect us.
[*At this point an angel dressed in dirty, tattered clothes strolls in and sits down, watching the man.*]

MAN: And Lord, for our oil reserves, and for the trees that Macdonalds is ripping out, and for the seals. Oh Lord, the list is endless, and so many people are being hurt by it all.

ANGEL: [*Cutting in.*] Yes, but do you really care, mate?

MAN: [*Suddenly realising the angel is there.*] What do you think you're doing in here? How did you get in? This is my home.

ANGEL: Wait a minute—I asked the question first, you ain't given me an answer yet.

MAN: I'm not interested in your questions; don't you know you're trespassing? I don't know how you got in here, but you're leaving right now. [*Takes the ANGEL's arm. He recoils from the smell.*] Ugh! You're in a right state, where on earth have you been?

ANGEL: Somewhere you've obviously never been, mush. That's what I'm on about, do you really care?

MAN: I don't think that's any of your business.

ANGEL: Exactly. Exactly. If you really cared it *would* be my business. I wouldn't have to ask you.

MAN: Who do you think you are—breaking in here like this?

ANGEL: You wouldn't believe me if I told you. I mean, I heard you—the environment, the ozone layer, the baby seals. Right—good! All very noble, I agree. But why? Why are you concerned—self-preservation, perhaps?

MAN: Because...because as a Christian I feel a certain responsibility towards the world, I suppose. I believe God tells us to look after these things.

ANGEL: So you're not doing it for me then?

MAN: What?

ANGEL: You're not praying for a better world for my sake then? You see, I don't think God calls you to look after the world. He calls you to love your brother, and if that involves the ozone layer all well and good. Otherwise—surely you're just looking after number one? That's why I say—do you really care?

MAN: Now wait a minute.

ANGEL: Sorry, mate, I think you're right. I shouldn't be here after all, I *am* in the wrong place.

MAN: Now you just listen, you don't come into *my* house to lecture me. I care, I do my bit, I do what I can.

[*They stare at each other. The MAN shrugs and turns away.*]

ANGEL: [*After a pause.*] Come with me now, then. I'll show you how to care.

MAN: What—now? Don't be ridiculous! I couldn't possibly. I've got responsibilities here. I need some rest. I've got a busy day tomorrow. I couldn't...I mean, we're not all called to do that, are we... I couldn't possibly go with you.

[*While he is talking, the ANGEL exits.*]

[*Seeing he is now alone.*] Hey, what's going on? Come back! We haven't finished the argument. You never told me where you came from.

ANGEL: [*Off-stage, over a PA.*] If I did—you'd never believe me.

[*The MAN looks around frantically. Freezes.*]

*Dave Hopwood*

# 45 Jack and the Dreamstalk

## THEME

The domination of self. This very simple sketch, involving narration and mime, was originally written for street theatre performance, but it could also work well in school assemblies or other indoor contexts.

## CAST

Two narrators, Jack, Jack's Mummy, a Giant and a group of about six, probably dressed in T-shirts and jeans.

## PROPS

The main prop is a stepladder at centre stage.

## SCRIPT

1: Once upon a time—
2: There was a nice little lad who lived in Sheffield—
1: In a nice little house—
2: With his mummy.
1: His mummy.
2: How nice to have a mummy.
1: Lovely.
2: And he was called Jack and his mummy was called—
1: Mummy.
2: How nice to have a mummy.
1: Unfortunately, Mummy and Jack didn't get on together very well.
2: Because Jack was a lazy little—
1: [*Interrupting quickly.*] And Mummy got really quite annoyed.
2: Because Jack was a lazy little—
1: Mummy was getting very irritated indeed.
2: A lazy little—
1: [*Holding nose.*] Who got right up her nose.
2: [*Holding nose.*] 'Get out!'

1: [*Holding nose.*] 'How much longer are you going to be in there?'
2: [*Holding nose.*] 'I'm stuck!'
1: That was it. Jack was stuck.
2: He was stuck for a job—
1: An opportunity—
2: A door to the future.
1: But he wasn't stuck for ideas—he had lots of ideas.
2: Ideas about Jack, about what Jack was going to be.
1: Jack was going to get a good job.
2: Jack was going to do very well for himself.
1: Jack was going to impress people.
2: Especially the ones with influence.
1: Jack was going to get promotion, one way or another.
2: He was going to reach the top—
1: Somehow.
2: Anyhow. [*As he dreams, Jack is beginning to climb the ladder. He is surrounded by adoring crowds reaching up to him with cellphones, autograph books, cigars, pension plans, air-tickets, strings of American Express cards, etc. He waves royally.*]
1: Jack was going to become so important. He would set up his own business.
2: And show mummy what a meteoric superstar he was after all.
1: But first he had to get a job. [*The vision fades and Jack falls off the ladder.*]
2: The problem was, Jack couldn't really decide what he wanted to be.
1: He wanted to be—
2: A film star. [*Again he dreams of upward mobility, acting out the various options.*]
1: A cosmonaut.
2: A striker transferred for millions to AC Milan.
1: A world-famous writer—
2: Of sensitive and popular novels.
1: In charge of a bank,
2: With billions of noughts.
1: A creator of fashion—
2: With thousands of fans.
1: A hero.
2: An icon.
1: A billionaire!

2: Jack was a lad with so much potential.
1: But first he had to get a job. [*He comes back down to earth again.*]
2: So he left school—
1: And popped down to the Job Centre with Mummy's good wishes for his future career—
2: 'Stop the day-dreaming, our Jack, and shift thy great backside!'
1: 'Thanks, Mam.'
2: And would you believe it, Jack actually got a job!
1: [*Jack is handed a bucket and mop.*] Not a very good one—
2: But it was a start—
1: On the six-lane freeway of life.
2: He got his first wage packet—
1: The first rung—
2: Up the Dreamstalk.
1: And Mummy was very proud of Jack—
2: But Jack was very bored with Mummy—
1: As he moved up the Dreamstalk—
2: Leaving her a little speck in the distance—
1: Which she treasured very carefully [*Mummy clutches a piece of fluff flicked from Jack's sleeve.*]
2: Because it was all she was likely to get.
1: And Jack moved up. [*The ensemble create his possessions and family.*]
2: A car.
1: A bigger car.
2: A flashier car.
1: A couple of cars.
2: A wife.
1: A bigger wife.
2: A flashier wife.
1: A couple of wives.
2: A steaming great factory—
1: Right in the middle of Sheffield.
2: A chain of factories all around the world.
1: *Jack's world*
2: Of people he had impressed.
[*Ensemble and Narrators together applaud wildly and chant.*] JACK! JACK!
1: Jack had fulfilled his dreams, all of them—
2: And reached the top.

1: But at the top—
2: There was an ugly giant—
1: Called—
[*Narrators and ensemble shout together.*] JACK!
[*An ugly giant appears up the back of the ladder behind Jack and throttles him.*]

*Breadrock Theatre Company*

# 46 God's Love is Like

THEME

A look at different analogies that are used in the Bible to describe God's love.

CAST

NARRATOR.
1—a man.
2—a woman.

COSTUME

Jeans and T-shirts.

SCRIPT

[*1 and 2 stand with their backs to the audience.*]

NARRATOR: This sketch is about love.

[*Wolf whistle off. 1 and 2 wrap their arms round themselves and move their hands up and down their backs.*]

No, not that sort of love.

[*1 and 2 become lovestruck, self-conscious teenagers.*]

Or that sort of love. Look, will you let me get a word in edgeways?

[*1 and 2 look sorry and sit down.*]

Thank you. Now, let's start again. This sketch is about love. God's love. What is God's love like? How about a man

[*1 jumps up*]

who makes a statue.

[*1 starts moulding 2 into a teapot.*]

He takes time over it, and makes sure it is

exactly what he wants. The statue carries the mark of the sculptor. He looks at it and because he made it he loves it. [*Looks at 2.*] God's love is sort of like that, but not quite. [*Under breath*] He's a better sculptor, for a start.

[*1 looks offended.*]

Sorry!

[*1 and 2 freeze.*]

Let's try again. How about a man

[*2 steps forward.*]

and an animal.

[*1 becomes a gorilla.*]

Hmm...let's try a different animal, shall we?

[*1 becomes a rabbit.*]

No. How about a dog?

[*1 becomes a very soppy labrador.*]

I suppose that'll do. The man loves his dog, and the dog loves the man,

[*1 and 2 are soppy together.*]

even though the dog isn't quite housetrained.

[*1 cocks his leg on 2.*]

But the man still loves the dog anyway.

[*2 wonders why she ever bought the dog.*]

God's love is sort of like that, but not quite.

[*1 and 2 freeze.*]

How about a man

[*1 steps forward.*]

and his child.

[*2 becomes a screaming toddler.*]

The man wants the best for his daughter. He's never far away. He feeds her when she's hungry, he listens to her every word, and he never gets impatient.

[*1 tries to comfort 2 but fails and gets more and more*

*angry, eventually strangling her.*]

Ahem!

[*1 looks embarrassed and, with a false smile, cuddles 2.*]

God's love is sort of like that, but not quite.

[*1 and 2 freeze.*]

How about a man

[*1 steps forward.*]

and his wife.

[*2 puts hand through 1's arm.*]

The man loves his wife.

[*1 gives flowers to 2.*]

They listen to each other.

[*1 reads newspaper while 2 talks to him.*]

They enjoy each other's company.

[*1 and 2 argue. Freeze with 1's arms outstretched.*]

God's love is sort of like that, but not quite. [*Pause.*] I know. How about a man who is loved by God. Man hates God.

[*2 crucifies 1.*]

But God... won't... stop... loving... man.

[*2 hammers nails into 1's wrists in time with narrator. All freeze.*]

*Clive Gardner*

# 47 Fresh Bread

THEME

John 6:35.

CAST AND COSTUME

BAKER—a good-humoured person eager to sell his wares. He is a down-to-earth working man with a rolling voice. If possible, dressed in white baker's coat and hat.
JESUS—strong, with a message to bring, but always calm and in control. Dressed in brown casual clothes. Strong but calm voice.

SCRIPT

[*Enter BAKER carrying a basket of bread and offering it to all.*]

BAKER: Roll up! Roll up! Fresh bread! Still warm. Get it while it's hot. Roll up! roll up! Best bread in town. Hand made this very morning. Crisp rolls. Buy your crumpets here. Fresh bread. Get it while it's hot. Hand made this very morning.

[*JESUS gets up from audience and makes his way to the front.*]

JESUS: New bread! new bread! No need to feel empty again. Free to everyone.

BAKER: [*Louder.*] Roll up! roll up! Your old established baker. Best bread in town. Beautiful baps. Tins, devons, farmhouses and French sticks. From your local baker.

JESUS: New bread, free to everyone.

BAKER: [*Irritated.*] Buy from the only baker recognised by Egon Ronay. The only jam doughnuts in the good food guide.

[*JESUS arrives at front.*]

JESUS: New bread free to everyone. No need to feel hungry again.

BAKER: [*Angrily.*] Oi!

JESUS: Yes?

BAKER: Are you mad?

JESUS: No.
BAKER: Trying to put me out of business?
JESUS: No.
BAKER: Then why are you giving bread away?
JESUS: It's not really bread.
BAKER: You'll get us honest bakers a bad name. Just so I know when I tell the Trading Standards people: what's in it?
JESUS: Well, I am.
BAKER: [*Surprised.*] What?
JESUS: It's like this. The bread you make is very good...
BAKER: [*Relaxes.*] Thanks.
[*JESUS joins BAKER on stage.*]
JESUS: In fact, I had some of your bread for breakfast. But...
BAKER: Yes?
JESUS: Just four hours later I'm hungry again.
BAKER: [*Confused.*] Yeah, well, that happens whatever you eat.
JESUS: [*Reassuring.*] But my bread—I myself—can satisfy all your needs.
BAKER: What are you on about?
JESUS: Do you ever feel empty inside, apart from when you're hungry?
BAKER: [*Nods.*] Sometimes.
JESUS: A bit fed up, wondering if there's any more to life?
BAKER: A bit.
JESUS: That's the hunger I'm offering to deal with.
BAKER: Really?
JESUS: Yes.
BAKER: Then why don't you come right out and say that.
JESUS: Because people misunderstand. If I said, 'Have a bite out of me and I'll make your life what God meant it to be,' they wouldn't listen.
BAKER: How come you and God are on such good terms?
JESUS: I'm his Son.
BAKER: Wow! [*Pause.*] So you're saying, if I take you into my life you'll put it right and I'll never feel empty again.
JESUS: That's right.
BAKER: Your bread's good value isn't it?

*Stairs and Whispers Theatre Company*

# *C Bible Characters*

## 48 Joseph

THEME

The story of Joseph, selected from Genesis 37 onwards, told in three sketches.

CAST

Part 1—NARRATOR, JOSEPH and five of his brothers: JUDAH, SIMEON, LEVI, ISSATHAR and REUBEN.
Part 2—NARRATOR, JOSEPH, JAILER, BUTLER and GUARD.
Part 3—NARRATOR, JOSEPH and HELPER.

COSTUME

Preferably traditional. Otherwise T-shirts and jeans.

SCRIPT

*Part 1*

| | |
|---|---|
| NARRATOR: | The brothers huddled around the campfire. Night was falling and it was getting cold. Simeon and Levi returned to the campfire. |
| JUDAH: | What did you do with Joseph? |
| SIMEON: | [*With glee.*] We stuck him down that horrible stinking pit. [*Laughs.*] |
| JUDAH: | Great! |
| LEVI: | That'll teach him. |
| ISSACHAR: | It's only what he deserves. |
| REUBEN: | So what are we going to do with him now? |
| SIMEON: | [*Aggressively.*] Kill him! |
| ALL: | [*Aggressively.*] Yeah, kill him! |

JUDAH: Do him in.
LEVI: Finish him off.
ISSACHAR: Get rid of the dreamer.
REUBEN: Hang on. Let's just think.
SIMEON: [*With malice.*] Yeah, let's think how we can kill him.
REUBEN: No, let's think *why* we want to kill him.
SIMEON: 'Cos we hate his guts.
ALL: Yeah, we hate his guts.
REUBEN: No, let's think *why* we hate his guts.
SIMEON: 'Cos he's a creep.
JUDAH: Yeah, he's Daddy's favourite
LEVI: And Dad always buys him trendy new coats.
ISSACHAR: And all we ever get is hand-me-downs.
LEVI: He's such a show-off.
ISSACHAR: He really fancies himself.
SIMEON: And what's more, we hate his guts. Kill him!
ALL: Yeah, kill him!
NARRATOR: It didn't take long for the brothers to agree what they wanted to do with Joseph. Reuben tried again.
REUBEN: Just because he's Dad's favourite isn't a reason to kill him.
SIMEON: How about his stupid dreams, then?
JUDAH: Yeah, those stupid dreams where we're supposed to bow down to him.
LEVI: Yeah, and where Mum and Dad are supposed to bow down to him too.
SIMEON: We wouldn't have to bow down to him if he was dead. Kill him!
ALL: Yeah, kill him!
NARRATOR: The scene was beginning to turn ugly. [*All the brothers make ugly faces.*] Not that ugly!
REUBEN: But what would Dad say? Joseph is his favourite.
JUDAH: Yeah, he'd be very upset.
SIMEON: But he'd forget after a while.
JUDAH: Yeah, it wouldn't take him too long to forget.
JUDAH: A couple of months.
LEVI: Six at the most.
SIMEON: Kill him!
ALL: Yeah, kill him!

NARRATOR: Things didn't look too good for Joseph.
JOSEPH: [*A pitiful voice off-stage.*] Help! Help!
ALL: [*Shouting.*] Shut up!
NARRATOR: Reuben was desperate. He didn't want to kill Joseph. Suddenly he spied a group of Midianites in the distance. An idea jumped into his head.
REUBEN: Would you rather kill Joseph or make money out of him?
SIMEON: What do you mean?
REUBEN: We could sell him as a slave to those Midianites.
JUDAH: How much money could we make?
REUBEN: He's got to be worth ten pieces of silver.
SIMEON: [*With pride.*] Ten pieces of silver? He's worth more than that, he's my brother!
JUDAH: Of course he is.
LEVI: He's young, hard-working.
ISSACHAR: Good-looking.
LEVI: Great imagination.
SIMEON: We'll settle for no less than twenty pieces of silver.

*Part 2*

NARRATOR: Joseph was taken to Egypt and sold as a slave to a man called Potiphar. He was a nice guy. But his wife wasn't. She wasn't even a nice girl! She told lies about Joseph and said he'd done some wicked things, but it just wasn't true. Joseph had been framed, and it wasn't a pretty picture. Now he was sitting in jail wishing he was somewhere else.
JOSEPH: [*Sadly.*] I wish I was somewhere else.
JAILER: Yeah, I bet you do.
JOSEPH: Still, there's no point in crying over spilt milk.
NARRATOR: Joseph was a bit of a philosopher.
JAILER: [*Confused.*] But you haven't spilt any milk.
NARRATOR: The jailer wasn't a philosopher.
JOSEPH: No, I just mean that.... Oh forget it.
BUTLER: [*Waking up.*] Forget what? [*To Joseph.*] What did I forget? [*To Jailer.*] Who are you?

JAILER: I'm the jailer.

BUTLER: Oh yes, of course you are. [*Suddenly realising.*] That means I'm in jail!

JAILER: Yes, you've been here for a week.

BUTLER: [*Calmly.*] Oh yes, I remember. [*Panicking.*] I shouldn't be here, I should be back in my job working for... um... um... who did I used to work for?

JOSEPH: Pharaoh.

BUTLER: Oh yes. I should be back working for Pharaoh doing... um... what did I used to do for Pharaoh?

JOSEPH: You were his butler.

BUTLER: Oh yes. I should be butling for Pharaoh, whatever that is. Say, where's the other chap, you know, the... um... um.

JOSEPH: The baker?

BUTLER: Yes, where's the baker?

JAILER: They came and took him away last night.

BUTLER: Oh yes, that's what you said would happen when you explained his dream. And it's come true!

JOSEPH: That's right. You remembered. And do you remember what I said about your dream?

BUTLER: Um... give me a clue.

JOSEPH: Your dream meant that very soon you'll go back to Pharaoh and be his butler again.

NARRATOR: Just then there was a knock on the cell door [*Knock, knock.*] One of Pharaoh's guards came in.

GUARD: Pharaoh has decreed that the butler is to return to his job.

BUTLER: [*Jovial.*] Good for the butler.

JOSEPH: That's you—you're the butler.

BUTLER: Oh yes. Good for me!

GUARD: Right, come with me.

BUTLER: [*Turning to Joseph before going.*] Thanks ever so much for explaining my dream. I won't forget you... um... um... what was your name again?

*Part 3*

NARRATOR: Needless to say, the butler forgot all about Joseph until Pharaoh himself had a dream. Joseph explained Pharaoh's dream and was an overnight success. He was given a new job—Prime Minister—which basically means 'Boss'. It happened just as Joseph had told Pharaoh; there were seven years of loadsafood, followed by seven years of famine. Very soon into the famine people were getting hungry, but Joseph had stored up food from the good years and was busy sharing it out.

HELPER: Have you seen the queues out there this morning?

JOSEPH: Yes, they get longer every day.

HELPER: And the people look hungrier every day.

JOSEPH: Still, it's our job to feed them. It's one sack per person.

HELPER: But Joseph, some of them out there are foreigners!

JOSEPH: Foreigners get hungry too.

HELPER: But there's one group who are just a dirty bunch of sheep farmers from up North.

JOSEPH: I know, I saw them.

HELPER: Well surely we're not going to feed them?

JOSEPH: Oh yes, even a dirty bunch of sheep farmers from up North.

HELPER: But are you sure there's enough to go around?

JOSEPH: Listen, I've learned over the years what it's like to be hungry, turned away and forgotten. And with God's help I'm not going to do the same to anyone else.

HELPER: Yeah, I guess you have had things rougher than I have. I don't know how you coped.

JOSEPH: It wasn't easy, but do you know, all the time I just knew that God was sorting something out.

HELPER: Well he's certainly done that.

JOSEPH: Exactly, or I wouldn't be here to help all these starving people, including my own family.

HELPER: What do you mean?
JOSEPH: Well, that dirty bunch of sheep farmers from up North are my brothers.

*Trapdoor Theatre Company*

# 49 I Spy with My Little Eye

## THEME

Numbers 13:16–33—Faith in God will move mountains.

## CAST AND COSTUME

Moses (known as M), MESSENGER, both in some simple military uniform. Spies 1, 2 and 3, dressed suitably in spy gear.

## PROPS

Map, possibly have snatches of James Bond music available to play when spies enter.

## SCRIPT

[*Office scene. Enter Moses (known as M in this sketch!) studying a large map on the board.*]
[*Enter Messenger.*]

MESSENGER: Excuse me, sir.
[*M keeps studying the map.*]
They're here. [*No response.*]...M? Sir?
M: Yes. [*still pre-occupied with the map.*]
MESSENGER: Shall I have them sent in?
M: Yes. One at a time, thank you.
MESSENGER: Yes sir.
[*Goes off, brings on SPY 1.*]
[*Play James Bond music!*]
M: Ah, come in. What have you to report?
SPY 1: Well, M, it's an amazing land. So rich and fertile. Grapes the size of apples, apples the size of melons, melons the size of...
M: OK, anything else?
SPY 1: It's beautiful. Green lush grass, cool clear water, just like in a holiday brochure.
M: I see, and what about the people.
SPY 1: Ah...well...

M: Yes?

SPY 1: Yes.

M: Yes what?

SPY 1: Yes, there are people, sir.

M: [*Impatient.*] Really! So what are they like?

SPY 1: Er, well...perhaps one of the others could tell you. I mean I was just concentrating on the geography, the agriculture, the basic ecology of the land. Nothing specific in my orders about, er, people, sir.

M: [*To MESSENGER.*] Send in the next one.

MESSENGER: [*Shouts off stage.*] Next!

[*Enter SPY 2, suitably dressed, etc.*]

M: Report on mission just completed?

SPY 2: Yes sir. Fertile land. Very fertile land. Beautiful valleys, hills. Grapes the size of...

M: Yes, yes, yes; I've heard all about that. I want you to tell me about the people.

[*SPY 2 looks anxious at SPY 1, who indicates to SPY 2 to tell M.*]

Or have you only had orders to look at the land?

SPY 2: No sir. [*Looks worried.*]

M: Well then?

SPY 2: Powerful. Huge people. Giants!

M: I see. And their cities?

SPY 2: Like fortresses. And very large...well they have to be...on account of the people being so big, sir.

M: [*Looking at SPY 1.*] And do you agree with this?

SPY 1: Yes, sir.

M: But of course you were only looking at the geography.

[*SPY 1 looks suitably admonished.*]

[*To MESSENGER.*] Any others outside?

MESSENGER: Yes sir. One other.

M: Send him in.

MESSENGER: [*Shouts off stage.*] Next!

[*Enter SPY 3, suitably dressed.*]

M: Can you make me a report on your recent mission?

SPY 3: Yes sir. The land is very good. Lots of fine plants, plenty to eat, etc. The people are strong and so are their cities, but with the Lord on our side we can easily defeat them.

SPY 1: What! You must be mad!

SPY 2: Or blind!

SPY 1: Didn't you see those people? Their cities? They would eat us for breakfast!

SPY 2: [*Turns to M.*] We are puny compared to them, sir. Don't listen to him. The man's a fool.

SPY 1: He obviously needs his eyes testing.

M: Someone is wrong.

SPY 2: And it's him!

M: Now wait a minute. You all agree that the land is rich and fertile?

SPY 1, 2, 3: Yes sir!

M: And that the people are strong?

SPY 2: And big.

SPY 1: And giants compared to us.

M: [*Calming them down.*] Yes all right. Strong, big and giants.
[*Looks at SPY 3.*] Do you agree?

SPY 3: Yes sir.

M: But you reckon we can beat them?

SPY 3: Yes sir. I don't deny anything of what they saw. I saw it too. But we don't have to be afraid of them, if we rely on God... I suppose it all depends on how you see things, sir.

*Stewart Jones*

# 50 Remember Your Creator

## THEME

Youth and age, based on Ecclesiastes 12.

## CAST

Reader, who could be female.
An actor, preferably male, to mime the reading.
Two female mourners and one male mourner.

## COSTUME AND PROPS

The reader should be dressed in ordinary clothes and come from the congregation to read the above chapter from the Lectern. The mimer could be dressed in clean T-shirt and jeans. The mourners should wear black, perhaps rather accentuated.

A large chair should be placed in the chancel of the church before the start of the service, with a walking-stick beneath it.

## SCRIPT AND ACTION

The actors should be concealed from view, perhaps by a church pillar, before the reader begins to read. But as soon as the first verse begins, the mimer should spring into view, implying 'youth', but proceed to mime the effects of ageing as the text describes this. It is obviously very essential that reader and mimer practise together carefully beforehand, which may result in further actions than those suggested below.

Verse 3—Arms shake, legs bend (the walking-stick should be picked up from the floor), mouth could open for first time revealing gaps in teeth (several teeth having been previously blacked), a brief attempt to walk should be made, stretching an arm out as if partially blind.

Verse 4—Cup hands to an ear. Then sit down on chair and appear to sleep, but suddenly leap up as if startled.

Verse 5—Walking very delicately and nervously. A hand should be brushed through the hair. Finally the mimer should sink into the chair and appear to flop dead. The mourners should appear from a pillar and walk slowly round the figure in the chair till verse 7 has been read, when all 'freeze' till the end of the reading.

*Michael Botting*

# 51 Daniel

## THEME

Daniel in the lions' den. (Daniel 6.)

## CAST

Four people—1, 2, 3 and 4.

## SCRIPT

[*This is a rap-style sketch involving lots of action and jumping around.*]

[*Enter four people, backs to the audience. They start clicking their fingers for four beats, turn and begin, still clicking their fingers.*]

All: Now cast yourselves back to 580 BC
When the Israelites were led away in—captivity
There came one day when King Darius said:

4: I'm afraid, in the future, you must worship *me* instead!
[*All stop clicking.*]

2: [*Wimpy.*] Sir? Sir? What if someone refuses?

1, 3, 4: REFUSES? [*2 falls back into arms of 1.*]

4: Why, I'll tear him limb from limb! [*1 and 3 pull 2, then stop.*]

1, 3: We've done that!

4: Well [*perplexed*], I'll throw him in the fiery furnace! [*1 and 3 go to throw 2, but then say:*]

1, 3: 1...2...[*Drop 2.*] We've done that. What about...a hanging? A shooting? A stoning? A drowning? A stabbi—

4: [*Interrupts.*] I know. I'll throw him to the lions.

1, 3, 4: [*Drop and prowl.*] Hungry, hungry, very very hungry!
Hungry, hungry, very very hungry!
Hungry, hungry, very very hungry!
Grrr!

2: No!

1, 3, 4: No?

2: Yes!

1, 3, 4: Yes?

2: No!
1: I'm confused!
2: He refused!
1: Who?
1, 2, 4: Daniel! [*3 jumps up as Daniel.*]
3: Now, hey big brother, I heard what you said:
If I don't worship you I'll soon be dead.
But I want you to know, let there be no dispute—
I ain't gonna worship no (human) substitute.
1, 2, 4: So the king [*1 and 2 place hands on shoulders of 3.*]
Threw Daniel [*1 and 2 fling 3 back. 3 drops to floor.*]
Into the Lion's Den! [*1, 2, 4 drop down and prowl.*]
1, 2, 4: Hungry, hungry, very very hungry!
Hungry, hungry, very very hungry!
Hungry, hungry, very very hungry!
[*Pause.*] Dead! Dead! Very, very dead! Ugh! [*1, 2, 4 keel over.*]
3: [*Jumping up.*] In the Bible it says there's only one God.
Bow to another, you'll be dead as a dog.
All: So don't be a wimp, don't be a fool.
Serve God... that's cool! [*All exit, clicking fingers again.*]

*Carl Robinson and Gary Swart*

# 52 Jesus Heals a Man with Leprosy

## THEME

Mime sketch based on Matthew 8:1–4.

## CAST

Four males playing LEPER, MAN, JESUS and PRIEST.
A small crowd of both sexes.
NARRATOR.

## COSTUME AND PROPS

Traditional first century Palestinian. Small bell for leper.

## SCRIPT

[*It is assumed that this sketch will be performed in church where there are choir stalls facing one another in the chancel between the communion rail and chancel steps. Also that there will be clergy stalls between the ends of the choir stalls nearest the congregation. Top left and right refer to the far ends of the choir stalls east and west respectively. Bottom left refers to the end of the clergy stall near the congregation, where pulpit or lectern is probably situated. If your church design is different, then make appropriate allowances.*]

[*Opening music.*]

NARRATOR: The news of Jesus the Carpenter was spreading like a fire in Galilee. No one had ever heard words like his before. And no one had ever seen such things as he did. Wherever he went, you could be sure that the crowds would follow him. [*Music.*]

[*The crowd moves slowly across from top right over to top left, talking in mime as they go.*]

There was one man, however, who couldn't join in any crowd anywhere: I don't know what his name was. He was a leper, and so people didn't want to know him one little bit. They wouldn't be interested in what his name was or where he came from—he was a leper and that was enough—he must keep away from people. They didn't have any cure for leprosy way back when Jesus was on earth. If you had leprosy, you had to keep well away from everyone, and if you were walking along the road and someone was coming along towards you, you were supposed to draw in to the side of the road. You had to warn others that you had this disease by shouting out—'Unclean! Unclean!' Fancy—that was all you could really ever say to other people, 'Unclean! Unclean!' Sometimes a leper would warn others of his disease by ringing a little bell, and they would remember to keep well clear of him. This leper was an outcast. Nobody wanted to know him; occasionally people might remember to leave food for him at a recognised picking-up point, but otherwise he was just a sort of tramp. In his rags and dirt he would wander alone—alone and hopeless, incurable in a sort of living death. Unclean. Sad, wasn't it?

[*LEPER comes on from top right, with rags and bell, and moves dejectedly down between the choirstalls to the chancel steps, limping very slowly with a stick. When he gets to the clergy desk on the organ side he should lean against the desk with head in hands.*]

[*MAN comes round from the congregation's side, turns the corner by the desk and meets the leper. Ringing of bells, waving of arms, consternation, etc. and the MAN steers wide of the LEPER and goes to top right to join the crowd. The LEPER leans back dejectedly against the desk again, head in hands.*]

But on this particular day an unheard of thing happened. Suddenly. The leper joined the crowd. I suppose, you see, that every eye was on Jesus. There He was, speaking to the people in those unforgettable words—no one wanted to miss a thing, of course—and then, so

[*Crowd now moves into the centre between the choirstalls, listening to JESUS, who stands in the Communion rail entrance.*]

timidly, the man with leprosy came to the edge of the crowd. He listened too. At least that's how I think it may have happened. And then perhaps one person just sort of half-turned his head, and saw what he was standing next to. A leper! [*dramatic music*] You can imagine the reaction. How dare he come so close! Quick—get rid of him—find a stone someone—we can't have this! [*Music...*]

[*The leper joins the crowd, who all have their backs to the congregation, hands cupped to their ears, while Jesus mimes talking.*]

[*The crowd gradually notice the leper. Horror spreads, waving arms, throwing stones, backing away to each side, forming an opening through the middle.*]

But of course, with people backing away from the leper, a way would soon have been cleared for him to get to Jesus. Which was exactly what he wanted! [*Music*]

Jesus didn't throw a stone. The Bible verse says that He was moved with pity, and that when the leper knelt down in front of Him and begged Him to make him well, all Jesus had to do was just touch him as He said, 'I will; be clean.' [*Dramatic music*]

[*The leper shields his face, limps towards Jesus and kneels before him, head bowed.*]

[*Jesus puts his hand on the leper's shoulder.*]

In a flash the man was cured. He was as right as rain! He was told to go and report immediately to the priest, so off he went as fast as his legs would carry him. The priest inspected him, and found that he was indeed well from his sickness, and gave him a clean bill of health!

The leper, who was a leper no longer, could mix once again with all his friends. How happy he was! [*Music*]

[*The leper stands in awe. Begins to look at his hands and legs. Jesus points to the pulpit. The leper goes there and stands there with PRIEST, who should have been there from the start. The priest looks the leper up and down, looks at arms and legs, and nods his head once vigorously in time with a single note of music.*]

You can be sure that he told them who had made him well. You could hardly stop him talking now! Of course this made people more anxious than ever to meet with Jesus and to follow Him wherever He went; because He brings sunshine into any person's life.

[*The leper joins the crowd, showing his arms and legs. The crowd mime happiness, arms in air, cheering, etc.*]

[*Jesus leads the crowd off to the vestry.*]

[*Closing burst of music.*]

*Christopher Porteous*

# 53 A Quick Transformation

THEME

The Transfiguration. (See Matthew 17:1–8; Mark 9:2–8.)

CAST

PETER, JAMES and JOHN.

COSTUME

Traditional Palestinian costume or jeans and T-shirts.

SCRIPT

[*The scene is the mount of Transfiguration. The three disciples have just walked up the hill. They are fairly nervous. They relate to Jesus, but he is never seen by the audience. He should be imagined as several yards away from the disciples, as if he has led them up the mount, and is a little ahead of them.*]

PETER: [*Blows out his cheeks and rubs his hands.*] Well! This is all very nice, Lord—I mean, you know, just the four of us up here. You—me—them. Yes, it's all very...er...nice! Isn't it, chaps?

[*He looks to JAMES and JOHN for support. They nod awkwardly.*]

JAMES: Oh! Oh, yes, yes, yes. [*He nods repeatedly.*] Isn't it John?

JOHN: Oh...it's very...nice here. [*He shrugs at James.*]

PETER: Well, er...shall we do something then? A game of footie, or something?

JAMES: Peter, just be quiet will you?

PETER: Sorry! Only trying to make conversa— [*He stops in mid-flow.*]

[*JAMES and JOHN are no longer listening, but are staring at Jesus. PETER does the same.*]

PETER: Hey! What's going on? Look at that! Jesus' face...and his han—and who's that with him? Those

two guys dressed in white. Turn down the brightness a bit, will ya? Oh this is great! I thought this was just going to be a private do!
[*He stares in horror, and his mouth drops open.*] Good grief! Look! Loo...loo...look!

JAMES: }
JOHN: } [*Irritated.*] We *are* looking!

PETER: Well, say something.
[*All three look at each other then cry:*] Aagh!

PETER: [*Beginning to move around frantically.*] I know, let's er...let's do something.

JAMES: Oh sure. Brilliant idea. Let's play 'I spy' shall we? Something beginning with er... [*he looks at Jesus*] 'T'?

PETER: James, shut up. I know—I've got it. Let's build something!

JAMES: }
JOHN: } [*Amazed.*] Build something?

PETER: Yes. A house. Just here. For Jesus and er...them other fellas.

JOHN: Oh yes? And what do you suggest we build it with?

PETER: Okay, okay...a tent. Let's put up a tent for them.

JAMES: Are you crazy?

PETER: Well, a shelter then.

JOHN: What—a bus-shelter!

JAMES: How about a phone-box!

PETER: [*Stops and looks at them.*] Now you're being stupid.

JAMES: }
JOHN: } *We're* being stupid?

PETER: [*He strains as if listening.*] Hang on—shh, d'you hear that?

JOHN: What now? An approaching cement mixer, perhaps?

PETER: No! Listen....
[*They all listen.*]

PETER: There it is again.

JOHN: Yes, I've got it—a voice—

JAMES: [*Repeating what he is hearing*]: 'This is my own dear Son, I am pleased with him, listen to him.'
[*They all look around in amazement. Peter whistles.*]

JOHN: Not a lot you can say to that is there?

PETER: Well, I could er....

JAMES: } Shut up!
JOHN:

PETER: Oh!

JOHN: And '*listen* to him'.
[*All freeze, John pointing towards Jesus.*]

*Dave Hopwood*

## 54 Darkness Below

THEME

Jesus healing the boy with an evil spirit. (Mark 9:14–29.)

CAST

Narrators 1 and 2.
Jesus.
Three disciples (Peter, James and John), but preferably at least two to nine more.
Two teachers—ideally make the number match the disciples.
Crowd of four—could be any number within reason and space restrictions, the more the merrier! The crowd-members could also play the other parts below, but ideally use separate people.
Father, son, evil spirit (hiding behind son, and hanging on to him until expelled).

SCRIPT

| | |
|---|---|
| 1: | When Jesus |
| 2: | Peter |
| 1: | James |
| 2: | and John |
| 1: | joined the other disciples |
| 2: | after the Transfiguration, |
| 1: | they saw a large crowd there. |
| CROWD: | Gabble—gasp—grin—gawp! |
| | Gabble—gasp—grin—gawp! |
| 1: | Some teachers of the law were arguing |
| 2: | with the disciples. |
| TEACHERS: | Argey—bargey. |
| DISCIPLES: | Argey—bargey. |
| TEACHERS: | Argey—bargey. |
| DISCIPLES: | Argey—bargey. |
| 1: | As soon as the people saw Jesus |
| 2: | they were greatly surprised. |
| CROWD: | Gabble—gasp—grin—gawp? |
| 1: | And ran to him [*they mime running*] |

2: and greeted him. [*Shake fists.*]
1: Oy!
2: Where you bin all this time?
1: What are you arguing with them about? [*He knocks heads together.*]
2: Jesus asked his disciples.
1: And the disciples answered:
[*One puts finger to mouth, one shrugs shoulders, one scratches head.*]
2: But a man in the crowd said,
1: Teacher, I brought my son to you
2: because he has an evil spirit in him [*spirit appears from behind*]
1: and cannot talk. [*Spirit covers boy's mouth with hands.*]
2: Whenever the spirit attacks him [*it does so*]
1: it throws him to the ground [*it does so*]
2: and he foams at the mouth [*he does so*]
1: and grits his teeth [*he does so*]
2: and becomes stiff all over. [*They lift him up.*]
1: I asked your disciples to drive the spirit out
2: but they could not.
[*One puts finger to mouth, one shrugs shoulders, one scratches head.*]
1: Jesus said to them,
2: How unbelieving you people are! [*Everybody puts finger to mouth.*]
1: How long must I stay with you? [*Everybody shrugs shoulders.*]
2: How long do I have to put up with you? [*Everybody scratches head.*]
1: Bring the boy to me!
2: As soon as the spirit saw Jesus [*it sees him and yelps*]
1: it threw the boy into a fit [*it does so*]
2: so that he fell on the ground [*he does so*]
1: and rolled around [*he does so*]
2: foaming at the mouth. [*He does so, perhaps producing a foam sponge to stuff in his mouth.*]
1: How long has he been like this?
2: Jesus asked the father.

1: Ever since he was so high. [*Boy tries to get up, but father pushes him down again.*]
2: Many times it has tried to kill him by throwing him in the fire [spirit throws him one way]
CROWD: Crackle—crackle—frizzle—frazzle—burn. [*Mime fire.*]
1: and in the water [*spirit throws him other way.*]
CROWD: Gurgle—gurgle—swallow—wallow—drown. [*Mime water.*]
2: Have pity on us and help us, [*Father kneels before Jesus*]
1: if you possibly can!
2: It's not if *I* can, said Jesus,
1: it's if *you* can.
2: Everything is possible
1: for the person with faith.
2: I do have faith [*he tries to get up*]
1: the father cried out,
2: but not enough. [*He falls back to kneeling.*]
1: Help me!
2: Jesus noticed that the crowd was closing in on them.
CROWD: Gabble, gabble—gasp, gasp—grin, grin—gawp, gawp.
1: So he gave a command to the evil spirit:
2: I order you to come out of the boy
1: and never go into him again.
2: With a scream [*it screams*]
1: the spirit threw him into a bad fit [*it does so*]
2: and came out [*sulkily it hangs around in mid-field*]
CROWD: Off, off, off, off! [*He storms off.*]
1: The boy looked like a corpse [*one disciple taps him and shakes head, one takes pulse and shakes head, one holds feather by mouth and shakes head*]
2: so that everybody said,
CROWD: He is dead.
1: But Jesus said,
2: Oh no, he's not.
CROWD: Oh yes, he is.
2: Oh no, he's not.

CROWD: Oh yes, he is.
*[Jesus takes boy by hand, helps him rise and stand up.]*
CROWD: Oh no, he's not. Praise the Lord!
*[They leave.]*
1: After Jesus had gone indoors
2: his disciples asked him, privately,
1: Why couldn't we drive the spirit out?
2: There's only one thing can drive this sort out
1: and that's prayer. [*One disciple presses 'hands together'.*]
2: Prayer. [*Second disciple presses 'hands together'.*]
1 & 2: And more prayer. [*Third disciple presses 'hands together'.*]

*Lance Pierson*

# 55 Getting Out of the Hell of It

## THEME

Luke 16:19–31—The Story of The Rich Man and Lazarus.

## CAST

Two Narrators, Rich Man, Lazarus (a crippled beggar), and Abraham. Servants, Angels and wild dogs are extra according to availability!

## COSTUME

Probably traditional would be best with a purple robe for the rich man.

## PROPS

The central prop might be a dining table, which remains even though the action switches from earth to heaven, and which will help to emphasise the straightforward reversal of roles in the second part of the story. Other props are suggested by the script.

## SCRIPT

1: There was once a notorious vicar.
2: Who insisted on dining sumptuously each evening with his curtains drawn back.
1: So that through his lighted window, the poor of his parish might be strengthened, not by the food he was eating,
2: But by the inspiring sight of how a gentleman ought to live,
1: Silver candelabra and all.
2: A similar incident, centuries earlier, must have reminded Jesus of the well-known story of the rich man and Lazarus.
1: Which means, 'Whom God helps'.
2: The moral of the story was:
1: He who has been good on earth,
2: Will be blessed in the kingdom of the dead.

1: Imagine a large house, with servants, big windows and tall doorways, marble floors and silver candlesticks.
2: The home of a very rich man.
1: So rich that he didn't need to work.
2: So lazy that he paraded around all day in a purple gown
1: And find Egyptian underwear.
2: So greedy that he spent most of his time feasting himself,
1: Or sleeping it off,
2: And generally losing control of his calories.
1: Outside his front door, lying in the dust,
2: In what little shade the wall of the house provided,
1: Lay Lazarus... a cripple.
2: Day after day,
1: Hour after hour,
2: Minute by minute,
1: Begging from anyone near enough to hear him.
2: Shouting whenever he had the strength,
The only attention he got was from the flies
1: And the wild dogs that licked the sores on his body.
2: The sores showed through the rags of his clothing.
1: The rich man always had to step over Lazarus on his way to town.
2: But that cry,
1: 'Pity! Pity a poor cripple!'
2: Had become so familiar, the rich man didn't hear it at all.
1: He continued his daily banquets in full view of the beggar,
2: Whose condition, the rich man told himself, showed that here was a miserable sinner being punished by God.
1: So who was he to interfere with the justice of God?
2: He said, wiping his hands on a hunk of bread and throwing it carelessly under the table.
1: Lazarus watched every movement.
2: He saw where the bread landed, but of course, being crippled, he couldn't grab it before the dogs gobbled it up.
1: Not long after, Lazarus died.
2: Hardly a gasp, hardly a groan.
1: Certainly nothing to disturb the strawberry mousse being eaten nearby
2: A glorious flight of angels descended to bear Lazarus swiftly to heaven.
1: The rich man didn't even notice he'd gone.

2: His eyes were glued to some delicious little creme caramels
1: Winking at him from the table.
2: He was just about to pop one into his mouth, when he was interrupted by a sharp pain in his chest.
1: Aaargh!
2: [*Sharp intake of breath.*] Oooh!
1: Heartburn was commonplace,
2: Indigestion was like an old friend,
1: But these symptoms were unfamiliar:
2: A rolling of the eyes,
1: A churning of the stomach,
2: A clutching of the heart,
1: A falling off the chair,
2: And a thrashing about on the floor.
A few flowers
1: A small mention in the local paper,
2: But nobody really missed him.
1: The rich man was soon losing a few pounds in the scorching heat of hell.
2: The flames brought tears to his eyes
1: And sweat streaming from his brow.
2: From where he was melting, the rich man could twist round and look up a great distance
1: He could see a magnificent banqueting table.
2: And sitting at the right hand of someone who looked like Abraham, he could just make out... *Lazarus*!
1: All was light and cool and refreshing.
2: 'Father Abraham,'
1: He shouted.
2: 'Send that Lazarus down with some water to cool my tongue. This heat is driving me mad'
1: Abraham shook his head.
2: 'Son, remember that in your lifetime you had all the good things and Lazarus had all the bad things. In death, lack of love and godlessness are punished. Faith and humility are rewarded.
1: 'And besides,'
2: Abraham went on,
1: 'Between us there is a great chasm, eternally fixed, so that no one can cross in either direction.'

2: 'Well, at least send Lazarus to warn my five brothers about ending up in this hell of torment.'
1: 'But surely God's word is clear enough?'
2: Abraham replied.
1: 'Of course,' said the rich man, 'but they would be really impressed if someone came back from the dead.'
2: 'If what God has already revealed to them in his word has not brought them to repentance,'
1: Said Abraham sadly,
2: 'Then neither will they listen to someone
1: Who returns to them
2: From the dead.'

*Breadrock Theatre Company*

# 56 The Rich Fool

## THEME

A retelling of Jesus' parable in Luke 12:16–21.

## CAST

Narrators 1 and 2 tell the story while a small group responds to them with the action (and props) described.

## SCRIPT

| | | |
|---|---|---|
| 1: | Once there was | *[group look expectantly at 1 then 2.]* |
| 2: | A rich man | *[one of the group steps forward, smoking a cigar, thumb inside braces, very smug.]* |
| 1: | Who | *[rest of the group look from 1 to 2 as they present this big build-up]* |
| 2: | Was | |
| 1: | Very | |
| 2: | Very | |
| 1: | Very | |
| 2: | Very | *[By this time the group should look as if they're watching a tennis match.]* |
| 1: | Very | |
| 2: | Very | |
| 1: | Very | |
| | | *[Expectant pause. Group wait, mouths open.]* |
| 2: | RICH! | *[Group are exhausted.]* |
| 1: | He also had | |
| 2: | A lot of servants. | *[Man snaps his fingers, group become servants.]* |
| 1: | To wait on him, | |
| 2: | Hand | *[Polish his nails. Wash his hands.]* |
| 1: | And foot. | *[Polish his shoes. Wash his feet. React to smell!]* |
| 2: | Foot | |
| 1: | And mouth. | *[Moo! In background.]* |
| 2: | He had a large bank balance. | *[Man watches as others weigh and count his money.]* |

1: Large Rolls, [*Servant brings dish of rolls. Others look perplexed.*]

2: And a large wife. [*Girl hits him with rolling pin.*]

1: One day

2: He had a flash [*Group turn to 2, horrified. Man looks embarrassed.*]

1: [*Hastily.*] of inspiration. [*All look relieved.*]

MAN: I'll build bigger barns,

2: He said,

MAN: To store up all my money,

1: He said.

2: The servants thought this was a good idea.

ALL: Good idea. [*They are* not *enthusiastic.*]

1: So in came the builders, [*All turn, walk and whistle.*]

2: Who did what they were good at. [*All fall asleep.*]

1: But eventually they started to work. [*Hammer, drill, chisel in rhythm, stop as teabreak is called.*]

2: However, [*Stop. Look up expectantly.*]

1: This still wasn't big enough to store [*All look up and shake heads.*]

2: His wife [*All look frightened.*]

1: Or his money. [*Count money. Scratch head.*]

2: So,

1: Back came the builders [*Builders repeat sequence.*]

2: To build an even bigger barn,

1: With two

2: Tall

1: Storeys,

ALL: Once upon a time…

2: And a lift. [*All press button and go down to noise of lift.*]

1: And so the man was happy— [*Man smiles. Group is relieved.*]

2: At last! [*Leans back, supported by two of the group.*]

1: But just then, [*Group look surprised, except for rich man.*]

2: As his life was on the up, [*All stare upwards.*]

1: The price of gold was on the up, [*All count money.*]

2: And his lift was on the up, [*Press button on lift.*]

1: The hand of God

2: Came down [*Group clap once. Rich man is shocked.*]
1: On him. [*He dies into the arms of the group.*]

*Dave Hopwood*

# 57 The Prodigal Daughter

## THEME

Modern version of the famous parable in Luke 15:11–32.

## INTRODUCTION

Even though this features two daughters rather than two sons, there's nothing very original about the idea in this sketch of a modern-day version of the familiar story from Luke 15. However, there is a surprise in store for the audience when, towards the end of the piece, one of the narrators tries to change the ending. This serves to highlight the astounding truth of this parable—our heavenly Father's willingness to forgive us in spite of our disobedience and self-centredness.

## CAST

The FATHER; TRACEY and SHARON, his daughters; NARRATORS 1 and 2; various 'friends'; supermarket manager; landlord.

## SCRIPT

[*Two narrators stand at the back of the stage, one either side. NARRATOR 2 speaks in the style of a Radio 1 disc-jockey. NARRATOR 1, by contrast, is very much Radio 4. Appropriate action to be improvised throughout by actors. Our local references, for instance to Norfolk and the A11, can, of course, be changed to suit your own situation.*]

NARRATOR 1: We present the story of the prodigal daughter.
NARRATOR 2: Hang about. Shouldn't that be the prodigal son?
NARRATOR 1: [*Stage whisper.*] We're a bit short of male actors.
NARRATOR 2: Fair enough. Equal opportunities and all that stuff. What does it mean anyway?
NARRATOR 1: What?
NARRATOR 2: This 'prodigal' bit.
NARRATOR 1: [*Pretending to know, but not fooling anyone.*] Well,

you know, it comes from the Latin: prod- dig-all. It means, well, prodigal, I suppose.

NARRATOR 2: You don't know either, do you.

NARRATOR 1: Of course I do. [*Turns back on NARRATOR 2, takes out a pocket dictionary, quickly looks through the pages and reads in a knowing voice.*] It means—how can I put it?—sort of 'wasteful of one's means', um, 'squandering', 'lavish'—actually.

TRACEY: [*Calling from off-stage.*] Can we get on with it, please?

NARRATOR 1: OK. Scene one.

NARRATOR 2: This guy in Norfolk, right. He's a rich farmer. [*Father enters; mimes appropriately.*] Really loaded. Know what I mean? Big farm, acres of turnips, carrots, cabbages, oilseed rape, all that green stuff, right. Making serious money. You get the picture?

NARRATOR 1: The farmer had two daughters.
[*They enter as their names are mentioned, curtsey and greet their father.*]

NARRATOR 2: Tracey... and Sharon.

NARRATOR 1: They were both elegant, charming, talented, exceptionally beautiful.

NARRATOR 2: [*Gesturing towards Tracey and Sharon.*] Is this right?

NARRATOR 1: [*Stage whisper.*] We're a bit short of elegant, charming, talented, and exceptionally beautiful actresses.

NARRATOR 2: Fair enough.

NARRATOR 1: Our story commences one lovely summer's day in the idyllic setting of the family's Norfolk farmhouse. Skylarks were singing their merry tune high in the sky, the fruit on the apple trees was slowly ripening in the golden summer sun, cornflowers held their proud heads high along the hedgerows, and...

TRACEY: Get on with it... please!

NARRATOR 2: Right, the plot. [*The actors mime appropriately—it all happens very quickly.*] Tracey fed up with country life. In a sulk. Goes to Dad. Demands her share of the family fortune. Wants to go to

London to live her own life. Mega tantrum. Dad gives in. Sharon thinks it a disgrace. Tracey takes the money, makes rude gestures to Sharon [*not too rude, please!*], packs bags and makes tracks for the big city.

NARRATOR 1: Scene two. London. [*Father and Sharon leave stage. Tracey wanders around looking at the sights.*]

NARRATOR 2: The big city. Bright lights, trendy, where the action is, life in the fast lane. Discos, parties, filofax, all that stuff. You get the picture?

NARRATOR 1: Tracey soon settled into the high life of the big city. She made friends quickly—and spent her money with abandon to impress them. She threw a big party for all her new friends. [*Friends enter, mime disco.*]

NARRATOR 2: Free cokes and crisps all round. Disco music, flashing lights, hours of fun. Then goodnight, Trace, cheers, see yer.
[*The friends wave and exit; then come straight back on again.*]

NARRATOR 1: The next night she threw another party, although she was a bit worried when she checked her purse.

NARRATOR 2: Free cokes all round—but no crisps. Disco music, flashling lights, hours of fun. Then goodnight, Trace, cheers, see yer.
[*The friends wave and exit, then come straight back on again.*]

NARRATOR 1: The next night she threw another party. But her money was running out.

NARRATOR 2: Disco music, flashing lights, hours of fun. But no free cokes or crisps. Friends disappointed. Goodnight, Trace, cheers, see yer. [*They wave and exit.*]

NARRATOR 1: The next night she threw another party. But no one came. She wandered lonely through the dark streets of the big city. She checked her purse. She was broke. [*Tracey opens her purse, turns it upside down, one coin drops out.*]

NARRATOR 2: Well, nearly broke.

NARRATOR 1: She gave her last 10p to a deserving cause.

[*Tracey picks up the coin, leaves the stage and hands it to someone appropriate in the audience.*] She wandered back to the solitude of her flat in the Fulham Road and cried her way through the night. From here on it was downhill all the way.

NARRATOR 2: Fate had put the skids under Tracey's life.

NARRATOR 1: She took a job at a checkout in Tesco's, but got the sack for being late. [*Tracey dawdles across the stage, is confronted by an angry manager, looking at the time, who gives her a sack and signals that she is dismissed.*]

NARRATOR 2: Her landlord threw her out of her flat for not paying the rent. [*She wanders across to the other side of the stage, where the landlord confronts her—puts out a hand demanding payment. Tracey shakes her head. The landlord signals that she must go.*]

NARRATOR 1: The following week she slept in the sack under the Hammersmith flyover. [*Tracey curls up inside the sack in a corner of the stage.*]

NARRATOR 2: Life had taken a turn for the worse.

NARRATOR 1: Her sweet dream of freedom had turned sour.

NARRATOR 2: Hungry, miserable, homeless, penniless. You get the picture?

NARRATOR 1: Then suddenly Tracey comes to her senses.

NARRATOR 2: She's been a fool.

TRACEY: I've been a fool! [*She leaps up dramatically, looks resolute and begins to walk round the audience, on her way home.*]

NARRATOR 1: Even the women who pick the cabbages on her father's farm have a better life than this, she thought.

NARRATOR 2: Mega-regrets. Time for action, going-home-wise.

NARRATOR 1: Scene three. Meanwhile...

NARRATOR 2: Back on the farm. [*Father enters, takes position centre stage and looks out into the distance.*]

NARRATOR 1: As he had done every day since she had left home, Tracey's father gazed longingly down the A11, with the same old question running through his mind...

NARRATOR 2: Will they ever make it a dual-carriageway?

NARRATOR 1: [*ignoring this remark*] Will she ever come home again?

NARRATOR 2: [*sings*] 'Will she no come back again?'

NARRATOR 1: And then in the distance he saw someone approaching. [*Father reacts appropriately.*] Could it be? Surely not! Yes. It was! He called Sharon. [*Sharon enters.*] Come quickly! Look, our Tracey is coming home!

[*Tracey reaches the stage and approaches the father, who stands with arms open wide to greet her.*]

TRACEY: I'm sorry, Dad.

NARRATOR 1: The father opened wide his arms to greet her, and said...

[*During the next bit of narration the three actors on stage and NARRATOR 1 look taken aback, and gradually move towards and form a group around NARRATOR 2.*]

NARRATOR 2: [*forcefully*] How dare you come crawling back here after the way you treated us? You ungrateful little wretch. You had a decent home here, all that you could have wanted. And you walked out on us. Well, don't think you can just come home now as though nothing had happened. Oh no. You can just turn round and get back where you came from this moment. You took your money, you've had your chance, so just clear off.

NARRATOR 1: [*interrupting*] No! That's not right!

NARRATOR 2: Well, it's only what she deserves, isn't it?

SHARON: Quite right.

NARRATOR 1: [*checking the script*] But doesn't the father actually want to forgive her? Look, he's been longing for her to come home. He even wants to have a party to celebrate, because his lost daughter has been found.

SHARON: That's not fair!

NARRATOR 2: And quite unbelievable. You're not telling me that, after the way she's treated him, he's actually going to forgive her! Why would he do that?

# 58 The Dishonest Steward

## THEME

This parable is supposed to be one of the more difficult ones to interpret. The sketch goes for the most obvious interpretation—using money wisely. (Luke 16:1–9.)

## CAST

NARRATOR; Dowager LADY TEABAG; CRABSHAW, a dishonest steward; AMOS, the Head Gardener; GREASE, a chauffer; ROSE, a chamber-maid and MRS BROOM, a housekeeper.

## COSTUME

As traditional as possible. CRABSHAW must have a hat.

## PROPS

'Silver' spoons.

## SCRIPT

NARRATOR: Our story begins in the splendid residence of the Dowager Lady Teabag.

LADY TEABAG: Hello my dears, how lovely to see you all.

NARRATOR: That was Lady Teabag. This man is Crabshaw, her steward. He is a dishonest steward. [*Enter CRABSHAW with handful of silver spoons.*]

CRABSHAW: Lovely, lovely loot. Lovely silver spoons. I wonder if she'll miss them. No, she won't. Mind you, she'll have to use a fork to eat her soup tonight.

NARRATOR: Now Jesus told a story about a dishonest steward, and it went something like this.

LADY TEABAG: Crabshaw!

CRABSHAW: Oh, lawks. [*Hides the spoons under his hat.*]

LADY TEABAG: Where is that confounded steward? Crabshaw!

CRABSHAW: Did you call, your ladyship?

LADY TEABAG: Of course I called. Crabshaw, do you realise that I had to eat my lobster consomme with a fork tonight?

CRABSHAW: Really, your ladyship. I hope you managed not to dribble.

LADY TEABAG: Not easy, Crabshaw. Do you know why I had to eat my lobster consomme with a fork?

CRABSHAW: Er.... I give up.

LADY TEABAG: Someone has pilfered the entire set of silver spoons, Crabshaw.

CRABSHAW: The silver spoons, your ladyship?

LADY TEABAG: Yes, Crabshaw, they're lorst.

CRABSHAW: Not lorst, my lady!

LADY TEABAG: Yes, lorst. Not only lorst, but gorn!

CRABSHAW: You don't mean....

LADY TEABAG: Yes, Crabshaw. Lorst and gorn!

CRABSHAW: Lorst and gorn. How forlorn.

LADY TEABAG: Who can have taken them, Crabshaw?

CRABSHAW: I can't begin to imagine, your ladyship.

LADY TEABAG: Think, man, think!

CRABSHAW: Er... [*Takes off hat to scratch head. All the spoons drop out.*] Ah, that's torn it.

LADY TEABAG: Crabshaw! You! You villain! You fraud! You scoundrel! I'm—I'm speechless. You shall have to go. Pack your bags and leave at once. [*Exit.*]

CRABSHAW: Oh lawks, what am I going to do now? I'll never get another job. I shall be flung out onto the streets and left to starve, a poor old man without a friend in the world. Sob, sob.

NARRATOR: Poor Crabshaw was very upset. How was he to make ends meet? Suddenly he had an idea. He was the steward after all, and in charge of all her ladyship's money. He called in all the people who owed money to her ladyship for rent arrears, beginning with Old Amos, the Head Gardener.

CRABSHAW: Amos, my old trooper, don't you owe some money to Lady Teabag?

AMOS: Oh, arrr.

| | |
|---|---|
| CRABSHAW: | How much? |
| AMOS: | Oh arrr, that'll be two months' rent come last full moon o' yon September harvest. |
| CRABSHAW: | Ah. |
| AMOS: | Arrr. |
| CRABSHAW: | And how much would that, ah, come to? |
| AMOS: | Arrr, mmm, arrr, ten pound and two sacks of turnips. |
| CRABSHAW: | Well, just you make it five pounds and think no more about it. |
| AMOS: | What? You sure? |
| CRABSHAW: | Of course. |
| AMOS: | Hee, hee, just wait till I tell the missus. |
| NARRATOR: | The next was Grease, her ladyship's chauffeur. He was very pleased to have his debt reduced. |
| GREASE: | Thanks, guv. I'll buy you a drink sometime. |
| NARRATOR: | So was Rose, the chambermaid, and Mrs Broom, the housekeeper. |
| ROSE: | Thank you Mr Crabshaw. |
| MRS BROOM: | God bless you, Mr Crabshaw. |
| ROSE: | If ever you're in trouble, just let us know. |
| CRABSHAW: | I will. |
| NARRATOR: | This way the dishonest steward made sure that he'd have lots of friends to help him in the future. But when Lady Teabag heard about this, she was extremely angry. |
| LADY TEABAG: | Crabshaw, I'm extremely angry! |
| NARRATOR: | But then she stopped and thought. |
| LADY TEABAG: | No, I'm not. I think you've acted very wisely. If there's one thing I admire, it's prompt action in an emergency. |
| CRABSHAW: | Thank you, your ladyship. Can I have my job back, then? |
| LADY TEABAG: | Certainly not. You may be wise, but you're still a rogue. |
| NARRATOR: | And Jesus finished the story and said, Put your money to wise use, but not dishonest use. And be sure you know the difference. |

*Breadrock Theatre Company*

# 59 The Persistent Widow

## THEME

The need to be persistent in prayer, based on the widow and judge in Jesus' parable in Luke 18:1–8.

## CAST

Widow and judge, who can also play the two characters, 1 and 2 at the beginning of the sketch. A small group of two or three. Jesus.

## COSTUME

Traditional.

## PROPS

Newspaper, knitting.

## SCRIPT

[*Jesus (J) is either sitting down teaching a small group or just sitting alone, motionless. 1 and 2 walk in, already talking.*]

1: You ask him.
2: No, it was your idea.
1: Oh, all right. Lord, can you tell us about prayer?
2: Yes, Jesus, I don't understand it.
1: [*To 2.*] Wait a minute—I thought you said this was *my* idea?
J: What is it that you don't understand?
2: Well, how's it work?
1: And why is it that sometimes we pray and we get the answer, and sometimes we pray and we don't? What's the secret?
J: There's no secret. Just keep on.
[*Jesus sits down, as if the conversation is over. 1 and 2 remain puzzled.*]
2: Keep on? But for how long?
J: For ever. Don't stop. Always pray—and never give up.
1: But. . . .

J: [*Standing again.*] All right, let me show you. There was once a judge—a very corrupt judge. [*J positions 1 as the judge.*] He feared no one—certainly not God. [*Judge stands proud. Begins to read the* Financial Times.] Okay?
[*2 nods, watching closely.*]

J: And there was a widow. [*J positions 2 as the widow.*] A very poor widow, defenceless and alone. [*Widow expresses this.*] And one day she came to the judge, and said:

2: Hey you, judge. Yea, you with the funny wig. I've been wronged by a man, and I want justice.

J: The judge, however, ignored her.
[*Widow goes right up to him.*]

2: Did you hear? I want JUSTICE! [*Shouts this. Judge jumps.*]

1: Madam, go away.

J: But she didn't, she kept on.

2: Justice.

1: No.

2: Yes.

1: NO!

2: [*Launches into a long speech.*] But that's not fair, I've been wronged, wasn't my fault, how was I to know? What's the world coming to? I've been alone for twenty-seven years now and one day this fella comes knocking on my door, I didn't know him from Adam did I? Mind you, he had more manners than *you*, young man, but of course, me being me...

1: Madam.

2: So I said, 'Look at the price of bin-liners.' But would he listen? No. He was more interested in me dahlias. Course if I'd have realised that when my late husband left them to me, I'd never have had 'em restored. Cost me £27 and that was before metrication.

1: Madam, please! [*He is growing more and more distraught.*]

2: But *did* he listen? No. Of course, I blame the parents myself—always off to the wrestling, dinner in the oven, what's a poor boy to do? Well, I'll tell you.

1: That's enough!

J: And so she went on...and on...and on....

2: And if that wasn't bad enough, he said I had woodworm. 'Woodworm,' I says. 'And who are you to say I've got woodworm?' So then I says, 'Now look here young man, you're just like your father, his eyebrows were too close together an' all.'

J: Until—

1: MADAM! ALL RIGHT! I may not fear God or man, but you're driving me up the wall, woman. Yes, yes, whatever you want—YES!

2: So there's me—dahlia in one hand, bin-liner in the other, woodworm under me arm...

1: [*Shouts in her ear.*] YES! WHATEVER YOU WANT YOU CAN HAVE!

2: [*Looking at him with distaste.*] Young man, there's no need to shout. I'm not deaf.

1: I don't care—*I* will be if you don't stop. You've worn me out. Whatever the request. It's yours.

2: [*Realising she's won.*] Oh... thank you. And about time too! [*Freeze.*]

J: And if an evil judge like that will give justice because of this woman's perseverence, won't your Father in heaven—who is perfect—give *you* justice, if you keep on asking? And so my question to you is this: when I return, will I find that kind of faith in your lives?

*Dave Hopwood*

# 60 All or Nothing

## THEME

The retelling of the story of Ananias and Sapphira, based on Acts 4:31—5:11, and illustrating Luke 12:2–3.

## CAST

NARRATOR 1.
NARRATOR 2.
KING (non-speaking).
SUBJECT 1 / GUARD (non-speaking).
SUBJECT 2 / GUARD (non-speaking).
TRAMP / ESTATE AGENT (non-speaking).
LOYAL SUBJECT (non-speaking).
MAN (non-speaking).
WIFE (non-speaking).

## COSTUME

Traditional, or jeans and T-shirts.

## SCRIPT

NARRATOR 1: There was once a King.
[*KING and SUBJECTs enter.*]
NARRATOR 2: A wise King.
NARRATOR 1: A just King.
NARRATOR 2: All-seeing.
NARRATOR 1: All-knowing.
NARRATOR 2: But he was kind and generous.
NARRATOR 1: And he cared for his subjects.
NARRATOR 2: And his subjects were kind and generous.
NARRATOR 1: And cared for each other.
NARRATOR 2: They cared so much that they would sell their possessions.
[*SUBJECTS 1 and 2 give money to a TRAMP.*]
NARRATOR 1: And give the money to those in need.
NARRATOR 2: And the King was very pleased.

NARRATOR 1: One day,
NARRATOR 2: One of the King's loyal subjects
[*LOYAL SUBJECT enters with bags of gold.*]
NARRATOR 1: Sold some of his land
NARRATOR 2: And brought the money to the feet of his King.
[*LOYAL SUBJECT hands gold to King.*]
NARRATOR 1: And the King—
NARRATOR 2: Who was wise,
NARRATOR 1: Just,
NARRATOR 2: All-seeing,
NARRATOR 1: All-knowing,
NARRATOR 2: Kind
NARRATOR 1: And generous—
[*King distributes gold.*]
NARRATOR 2: Shared the man's gift
NARRATOR 1: Among those in need.
NARRATOR 2: And the King was very pleased.
NARRATOR 1: Then there was another of the King's subjects
NARRATOR 2: And his wife.
NARRATOR 1: And the man said
NARRATOR 2: To his wife,
NARRATOR 1: 'Let's sell our field and give the money to the King.'
NARRATOR 2: And his wife said,
NARRATOR 1: 'Why?'
NARRATOR 2: 'Because then'
NARRATOR 1: Said the man
NARRATOR 2: 'The King will be pleased with us.'
NARRATOR 1: 'Oh,'
NARRATOR 2: Said the wife.
NARRATOR 1: 'It must be worth at least...'
NARRATOR 2: 'Phew! At least!'
NARRATOR 1: 'Well...quite a bit!'
NARRATOR 2: And so they decided
NARRATOR 1: That if they gave 'quite a bit' to the King
NARRATOR 2: He would be very pleased.
NARRATOR 1: So an Estate Agent came.
[*ESTATE AGENT enters.*]
NARRATOR 2: He looked at the field,
NARRATOR 1: Walked on it,
NARRATOR 2: Measured it,

NARRATOR 1: And calculated
NARRATOR 2: That it was worth...
NARRATOR 1: Phew! At least...
NARRATOR 2: Well...quite a bit.
[*ESTATE AGENT hands over wad of banknotes.*]
NARRATOR 1: And quite a bit more!
NARRATOR 2: In fact, twice as much.
[*ESTATE AGENT hands over another wad of banknotes. He exits.*]
NARRATOR 1: 'Well!'
NARRATOR 2: Said the man.
NARRATOR 1: 'Won't the King be pleased with us!'
NARRATOR 2: And as they thought of how pleased the King would be
NARRATOR 1: They began to think about the money
NARRATOR 2: And all the things they needed.
NARRATOR 1: Well, not exactly 'needed'—
NARRATOR 2: More 'could do with'.
NARRATOR 1: Like a Nicam digital stereo alarm-clock
NARRATOR 2: With a built-in teamaker, optional radio and snooze button.
NARRATOR 1: Or a remote control, long-play videotape recorder
NARRATOR 2: That can copy thirty-two hours worth of programmes from four different channels at once.
NARRATOR 1: And that sort of thing.
NARRATOR 2: And after they'd thought of all these things
NARRATOR 1: They decided that the money should still be given to the King.
NARRATOR 2: At least,
NARRATOR 1: Quite a bit of it.
NARRATOR 2: But the 'bit more'
NARRATOR 1: They would hang on to.
NARRATOR 2: That way the King would be pleased with them
NARRATOR 1: And they could still buy the things they needed.
NARRATOR 2: Well, not exactly 'needed'—
NARRATOR 1: More 'could do with'.
NARRATOR 2: So, while his wife went on a shopping spree
[*WIFE exits.*]

NARRATOR 1: The man went to the King.
*[KING and GUARDS enter. MAN approaches them.]*
NARRATOR 2: 'I have sold my field for quite a bit.'
NARRATOR 1: He said,
NARRATOR 2: And laid the money at the King's feet.
NARRATOR 1: And the King—
NARRATOR 2: Who was wise,
NARRATOR 1: Just,
NARRATOR 2: All-seeing,
NARRATOR 1: All-knowing—
NARRATOR 2: Said,
NARRATOR 1: 'Why do you pretend to give me everything
NARRATOR 2: When you have kept back just as much?
NARRATOR 1: Would it not have been better
NARRATOR 2: To have given all or nothing
NARRATOR 1: Instead of lying?'
NARRATOR 2: And he ordered the man to be carried out
NARRATOR 1: And banished from the Kingdom.
*[GUARDS swiftly carry man out.]*
NARRATOR 2: Then the King said,
NARRATOR 1: 'Nothing is covered up that will not be revealed,
NARRATOR 2: Or hidden that will not be known.'
*[The GUARDS return.]*
NARRATOR 1: Three hours later
NARRATOR 2: The man's wife returned.
*[WIFE enters.]*
NARRATOR 1: She went to the King,
NARRATOR 2: Expecting him to be very pleased.
NARRATOR 1: Instead the King asked,
NARRATOR 2: 'How much did you receive for your field?'
NARRATOR 1: 'Quite a bit,'
NARRATOR 2: Said the wife.
NARRATOR 1: Then the King said,
NARRATOR 2: 'Why did you agree with your husband to do this?
NARRATOR 1: Did you not realise that you cannot hide anything from me?'
NARRATOR 2: And he ordered her to be carried out

NARRATOR 1: And banished from the Kingdom.
[*GUARDS swiftly carry her out.*]
NARRATOR 2: Then said the King—
NARRATOR 1: Who was wise,
NARRATOR 2: Just,
NARRATOR 1: All-seeing,
NARRATOR 2: And all-knowing—
NARRATOR 1: 'Whatever you have said in the dark shall be heard in the light,
NARRATOR 2: And what you have whispered in private rooms shall be proclaimed upon the housetops.'
NARRATOR 1: And the people were afraid.
NARRATOR 2: But the King was kind and generous,
NARRATOR 1: And the people remembered his words.
NARRATOR 2: And the King was very pleased.

*Robert Meadwell*

# *Bibliography*


Paul Burbridge and Murray Watts,
*A Time to Act*, Hodder, 1979.
*Lightning Sketches*, Hodder, 1981.
*Red Letter Days*, Hodder, 1986.

John Bell and Graham Maule,
Wild Goose Publications 1-6. Sketches from the Iona Community full of humour and straight to the point.
1. *Life and Teaching of Jesus*
2. *Death and Forgiveness. Jesus answers questions*
3. *Old Testament*
4. *Lent and Easter*
5. *Parables of Jesus and Paul*
6. *Advent and Christmas*
*Eh Jesus... Yes Peter...?* Volumes 1-3. Dialogues between Jesus and Peter, where Peter is asking most of the questions.

Margaret Dean (Ed), *Pick and Mix* Church House Publishing, 1992. Learning and worship Ideas for all ages.

Maggie Durran, *All Age Worship*, Angel, 1987.

Nigel Forde, *Theatrecraft*, MARC, 1986.

John Finney, *Finding Faith Today*, Bible Society, 1992.

Derek Haydock,
*Acts for Apostles*, Church House Publishing, 1987.
*Drama for Disciples*, Church House Publishing, 1988.
*Plays on the Word*, Church House Publishing, 1993.
*Sketches from Scripture*, Church House Publishing, 1991.

Dave Hopwood, *Child's Play, Short & Snappy, Stage Right* available from 5 White Rose Lane, Woking, Surrey GU22 7JA.

Graham Jeffrey, *The Gospel According to Barnabas*, Kevin Mayhew, 1975. Other 'Barnabas' titles available from KM Rattlesden, Bury St Edmonds, Suffolk IP30 0SZ.

Andy Kelso, *Drama in Worship*, Grove Books, 1975.

Michael Perry, *The Dramatised Bible*, Marshall Pickering/Bible Society, 1989.

Paul Simmonds, *Reaching the Unchurched*, Grove Books, 1992.

Judy Gittis Smith, *Show me!* Creative Resources Bible Society. A must for anyone using drama with 3-13s.

Geoffrey and Judith Stevenson, *Steps of Faith*, Kingsway, 1984. Excellent book on mime and dance.

Steve Stickley & Alan MacDonald, *Drama Recipe Book*, Minstrel, 1989.

with Philip Hawthorn, *Street Theatre*, Minstrel, 1991.

Steve and Janet Stickley, *Footnotes*, Hodder, 1987.

with Jim Belben, *Using the Bible in Drama*, Bible Society, 1980.

Murray Watts,

*Christianity and the Theatre*, Handsel, 1986.

*Laughter in Heaven*, MARC, 1985.

# *Index of Texts*

# *Index of Themes*